MICRO FINANCE FOR DEVELOPMENT OF FISHERMEN

MICRO FINANCE FOR DEVELOPMENT OF FISHERMEN

By

Dr. Rabi Narayana Misra

&

Dr. I.P. Sahu

DISCOVERY PUBLISHING HOUSE PVT. LTD.

NEW DELHI-110 002

Published by:
Tilak Wasan
DISCOVERY PUBLISHING HOUSE PVT. LTD.
4831/24, Ansari Road, Prahlad Street
Darya Ganj, New Delhi-110002 (India)
Phone: +91-11-23279245, 43764432
Fax: +91-11-23253475
E-mail: parul.wasan@gmail.com
info@discoverypublishinggroup.com
web: www.discoverypublishinggroup.com

***First Edition:* 2011**
ISBN: 978-81-8356-713-8

Micro Finance for Development of Fishermen

Printed at:
Shree Balaji Art Press
Delhi

Preface

The economic and social goal of our national policy has concentrated on socialism based on the welfare state, mixed economy and planning. It aims at the realization of the social objectives spelt out in the Directive Principles of State Policy. The concept of welfare state, therefore, has been the recurring slogan of our legislators and administrators. The socio-economic implications of the existing institutional structure requires to be studied. In this respect the banking sector has been playing an important role for developing the economic condition of the people at large. However, there are many who are yet to receive the careful consideration of the banking sector. As against this our chief concern is to show the impact of our policy on the economic development of those people who are now being considered as a neglected community. The present study has, therefore, opted the fishermen community living in the coastal belt in Ganjam district and engaged in fishing trade in its inland areas. It is also felt that different financial institutions, money-lenders, sahukars etc. have an impact on the life pattern of these people.

The present book has been divided into two parts. In the first, a theoretical review is made on the basis of available literature and in the second part of book empirical analysis is made on the basis of collected data from the field study of Ganjam district with a fishery population and the fishery population of Orissa. The fishery population of Ganjam constitutes three per cent of the total population. Hence, their socio-economic and financial problem needs to be studied.

Fishery is now a popular business in different parts of the district where not only fishermen but also people belonging to different castes, creeds and colours are also engaged. However, in the coastal belt 'Noliyas' are the dominating community who are taking keen interest in marine fishing. It is not out of place to mention that an exhaustive study of fishing industry is found in the country as a whole. The historical development of the trade in Ganjam district is also traced and analysed. It also studies how the liberalized policy of the government in the banking sector has affected people for developing a favourable attitude. In 22 blocks and one Notfied Area Council Gopalpur it is found that fishing has become one of the means of livelihood, though it causes a lot of hardship to them. Interestingly, marine fishing, now a very popular business despite difficulties on the part of those engaged in this trade has invited the attention of the investigator to make a detailed study and analyse the related data with regard to it. The part played by different commercial banks such as State Bank of India, Andhra Bank, Punjab National Bank, Uco Bank etc. has been exhaustively dealt with numerically.

The present study is expected to throw light on various aspects of fishermen, actively engaged in fishing business. The development of this community will influence the socio-economic condition of the district in particular and the State in general.

Rabi N. Misra
I.P. Shau

Acknowledgements

My wife Smt. Swarna Prava Misra has taken all positive steps for writing this book. My son Sri Roopesh and Rookesh along with my daughter-in-law were taken all efforts for editing this book. So I am very much thankful to them.

I convey my heartful thanks and express my warm gratitude to Mr. Tilak Wasan, Director of Discovery Publishing House Pvt. (Ltd.), Ansari Road, New Delhi for publishing this book without any hesitation. I am also thankful to his son Mr. Parul Wasan and other staff members of Discovery Publishing House those who are actively involved in publishing the book in time.

Dr. I.P. Shau

Contents

List of Abbreviation

ADF	:	Assistant Director of Fisheries
AIS	:	Accidental Insurance Scheme
BWFDA	:	Brackish Water Fishery Development Agency
BLC	:	Beach Landing Craft
BOBP	:	Bay of Bengal Programme
BPL	:	Below Poverty Line
CBFM	:	Community-based Fisheries Management
CIFA	:	Central Institute of Freshwater Aquaculture
CPR	:	Common Property Resources
CFCMS	:	Central Fishermen Co-operative Managing & Processing Society
DFPR	:	Department of Fisheries and Panchayat Raj
DFDI	:	Department for International Development
DOD	:	Department of Ocean Development
DOF	:	Directorate of Fisheries
DRDA	:	District Rural Development Agency
FEZ	:	Exclusive Economic Zone
EPW	:	Economic and Political Weekly
FAO	:	Food and Agricultural Organisation
FRP	:	Fibre Re-inforced Plastic
FSI	:	Fishery Survey of India
FFDA	:	Fish Farmers Development Agency
FISHFED	:	The Orissa State Fisheries Co-operative Federation Ltd.

GDM	:	Ganjam District Manual
GO	:	Government of Orissa
GSDP	:	Gross State Domestic Product
GOI	:	Government of India
GIC	:	General Insurance Company
H_2	:	Hectares
IBE	:	In Board Engine
ICE	:	Integrated Coastal Management
IOC	:	International Oceanographic Commission
IRY	:	Indira Rojagar Yojana
IRDP	:	Integrated Rural Development Programme
IRE	:	Indian Rare Earth Limited
JRY	:	Jawahar Rozgar Yojana
km	:	Kilometre
LIC	:	Life Insurance Corporation of India
m	:	Metre
MPEDA	:	Marine Products Export Development Authority
MASD	:	Mahila Sanchayika Sangha
MEO	:	Marine Extension Officer
MBM	:	Materials Balance Model
MEY	:	Maximum Economic Yield
MPCE	:	Monthly Per Capita Expenditure
MIP	:	Minor Irrigation Point
MPCI	:	Monthly Per Capita Income
MSY	:	Maximum Sustainable Yield
MS	:	Mission Shakti
MT	:	Metric Ton
NFF	:	National Fishermen's Forum
NABARD	:	National Bank for Agricultural and Rural Development of India

NGO	:	Non-Government Organisation
NCDC	:	National Co-operative Development Corporation
OPDC	:	Orissa Pisciculture Development Corporation
ODA	:	Overseas Development Administration
ODG	:	Orissa District Gazette
OFDC	:	Orissa Fisheries Development Corporation
OMFRA	:	Orissa Marine Fisheries Regulation Act
PHC	:	Primary Health Centre
PFCS	:	Primary Fishermen Co-operative Societies
PHF	:	Post-Harvest Fisheries
PCFCS	:	Primary Chilika Fishermen Co-operative Society
PIFCS	:	Primary Inland Fishermen Co-operative Society
PREM	:	Peoples Rural Education Movement
PMFCS	:	Primary Marine Fishermen Co-operative Society
RLTAP	:	Revised Long-term Action Plan
RBI	:	Reserve Bank of India
RGB	:	Rusikulya Gramya Bank
STEP	:	Support to Training and Employment Programme for Women
SGSY	:	Swarnajayanti Gram Swarozgar Yojana
SGRY	:	Sampoorna Gramin Rojgar Yojana
S.D.	:	Sustainable Development
SHG	:	Self-helf Group
SLBC	:	State Level Bankers Committee
Sq	:	Square
SBI	:	State Bank of India

TRYSEM	:	Training of Rural Youth for Self Employment
TEK	:	Traditional Ecological Knowledge
TMT	:	Thousand Metric Ton
UNO	:	United Nations Organization
UBI	:	United Bank of India
UAA	:	United Artists Association
UNGP	:	United Nations Development Programme
WTO	:	World Trade Organisation

Chapter 1

Introduction and Methodology

Introduction

From pre-historic period fishes have been used as protein-rich diet for human beings. The popularity of fishes has been mentioned in our religious literature like the Ramayana and the Mahabharata. In West Bengal, Bihar and Orissa the fish industry is about 1500 years old. In Bengal, every family has at least one pond for fish. It can propel and balance itself with the help of fins. It is a blind belief that if *Labeo rohita* fish in particular is offered during the *Sradha* ceremony, the dead person will certainly go to heaven. There is also another view that human race originated near the water reservoir and the fishes might have attracted the human beings. Fresh water fishes provide valuable source of food supply to the inhabitants of the countries located in tropical regions.

In America the fishes of great lakes have considerable economic importance. Flesh of fish is a highly perishable commodity and the composition constitutes 60-80 per cent of water, 13-20 per cent of protein and greater or lesser amount of fat. The fish also contains phosphorus and Vitamins.

Fisheries, including aquaculture provides an important source of protein food, employment, trade and economic well-being for the present and the future generation.

The wealth of aquatic resources was assumed to be an unlimited gift of nature. With increased knowledge and dynamic development of fisheries after the world war II the myth has faded. It is realised that aquatic resources, although renewable and exhaustable are not infinite and thus need to be properly managed. The belief that food from land resources will be able to support the ever-increasing population is relatively becoming 'Paradoxical' as 'Malthusian pessimism' prevails in many parts of the world. In the context of rapid growing human population and increasing protein malnutrition, food security assumes greater significance in the developing countries.

The problem of 'protein gap' at present is more acute. The shortage of conventional food aggravates the problem. Producing more seafood from the sea can fill up the protein deficiency. The fish available in large quantities in the oceans would be able to meet the nutritional requirement of the mankind.

The exploitation of the marine fish resources can definitely support not only the present population but also a bigger population of the world. It is estimated that 46 million tons of fish could be adequate to supplement the diets of 6 billion people provided it is shared equally.

The marine fisheries have been playing an important role for the national economy. It also generates a good source of food and rural coastal employment as per the declaration of Exclusive Economic Zone (EEZ) in 1910. The potential of these resources has become more apparent in successive developmental plans of the Central and State Governments which have emphasized on the importance of increasing fish production and export promotion.

There are about 30,000 to 40,000 species which differ widely from each other in shape, size, habit, and habitats. Some of them are very small not more than an inch in length while a few others attain a length upto 18.50 meter. They live in seas, rivers, lakes, canals, dams and almost every place where there is water. Fishes have usually a streamline body. Some are elongated snake like and a few are dorsal compressed. They have paired and unpaired fins supported by soft or spiny rays. They constitute economically a very important group of animals. Besides being used as a good food, fish lever is an important source of oil containing vitamin A and D. Body oil from fish is extensively used in shop industry and tanning.

History of Fisheries

Fisheries and agricultural farming have evolved simultaneously in the history of human civilization. Interest in fish eating dates back to the dawn of history. It is believed that hunting for fish was not uncommon in pre-historic times. Near a river or lake or cave dwellers of the old stone age (4000 BC) heaps of shell fish and sea fish have been found. The great distance by which these sites were separated from the sea points out some primitive way of fish preservation like sun-drying and smoke-drying over the wood fire. It was practised by these ancient dwellers to keep the food in edible condition. New Stone Age (10,000 BC) has also given evidence of salmon smoking practices. Bronze Age (3500 BC) was the time when salting offish started. Trading in dried fish, of course, was in vogue with ancient civilization of Egypt, Mesopotamia and Indus valley. Many cities were christened according to their fishery activity viz. Sidon (meaning fishermen's town and Malaga (meaning the salting town) in the Mediterranean. Among the Greeks and the Romans, fish became an important food of the rich and the poor. Iron Age (1000 BC) saw the great trades in dried, smoked and salted fish in Greece. It was during 400 BC to AD 450 a highly organized fishery emerged in the Roman Empire. In the middle age (AD 500 to AD 1500), fishing activity was more pronounced in the Atlantic and gained importance. The empirical finding of the preservation methods like salting, drying, smoking and poking in vinegar of the medieval times have come down to the present time. It was not until the beginning of the 18th century that preservation in ice was started. The Chinese were the first to use ice in preserving the fish during transport. Ice preservation of fish was introduced in England in 1786. Nineteenth century brought the time of scientific consideration. Application of science in agriculture by the middle of the 19th century led to agriculture outpacing the fishery industry. However, the application of science in fishing industry was made in recent times; Shore fishing, deepsea fishing and fish culture hold enormous promise. The interest in the nutritive value of fish was first keenly taken when there occurred a sudden scarcity in the post World War I. In twenties and thirties the discovery of Vitamin A and D placed fish in prominent as it is rich in vitamin.

Relevance of the Study

After globalisation technology has played an important role to utilize the land resources at optimum level to produce food grains and we are now self-sufficient with regard to food. But a balanced diet, which is highly required for a common man still lags behind. Thus, fish has played an important role and nearly 60 per cent of the people are very fond of fish. For this purpose, we want to use sea resources, which is quite natural and which covers 70 per cent of the global area. Fishing business is one of the oldest profession of the society. Due to lack of technological know how the fishermen use traditional method for collection of fish. Use of modern technology, proper education to fishermen can turn fishing industry as the leading industry of the country and earn huge foreign exchange in the present era.

The coastline of Orissa covers around 480 kilometre ana fishermen's population in the state as per the latest census is 8.02 lakh. Similarly, Ganjam district has coastline of 60 km having 93,686 fishermen as per 2001 census.

The 'fishermen cult' is a very old tribe and the entire sea is at their disposal. The sea will not betray them financially and it is but natural that they can also develop their standard of living as their counterpart in the agricultural sector.

The fishermen are still very poor and illiterate. They have no social status. Though they play a significant role in providing nutritious food like fish, they are still treated shabbily. In order to improve their economic condition. Steps are being taken to protect fishermen from the clutches of the landlords and Shaukars. They are yet to use more and more crafts, gills, and other fishing equipments for which finance plays a major role.

In this scenario it needs consideration to improve the standard of living of the fishermen in the sample district in particular and the state in general. The state can gain economic advantage in the form of foreign exchange by exporting prawn, marine fish, estuarine, deltic and riverine fish.

The financial constraint is a major obstacle to their inability to live a decent living standard. Further, an attempt has been made to find out how much financing is necessary to improve their standard of living. Thus, the fishermen community needs finance for better living condition.

As financial institutions and non-financial institutions play an important role in financing poor fishermen of the district, it has been decided to conduct in-depth study on this burning problem on utilization of natural resources like use of sea by fisherman. So the investigator has decided to take up the study in marine fishing with inland fishing and suggest measures which will be of some use to the Government.

Review of Literature

In the field of fisheries various scholars have made their studies at different times.

Sahu, Purussottam wooly in his titled "Marine Fishing and sustainable development of the Fishermen in Ganjam District, Orissa" (2004) has made an attempt to analyse various aspects of marine fishing. He also dealt with fishing technology, marketing structure and fisheries management. He observes that growth of marine fish catch in Ganjam district is slow and marketing is not done properly. He has drawn a very gloomy picture of the socio-economic condition of the fishermen community living in different part of the district and suggested proper remedial measures to be taken to uplift their living conditions. But Mr. Sahu has not made any attempt regarding the rate of socio-economic changes of fishermen in Ganjan district after availing the finance from different institutions or agencies.

Aleyamma, Issac in his work titled, "The Economy of the Marine Higher women in Ganjam District in Orissa" (2000) has made an attempt regarding the study of various problems that are related to fishermen and suggested how to improve their standard of living. Moreover, he dealt with how the fishermen are faced with many problems like literacy, child marriage, alcoholism, cyclone etc. The author has further emphasized that their life is more interlinked with ecology compared to their counterparts living in other places. But he has remained silent about the financial aspect of their life.

Bala, Supriya in her study titled "Economics of Marine Fisheries in Onssa" (1999) tries to make an attempt on economic analysis of marine fisheries in Orissa. The marine fishing sector deals with traditional sector, modern sector and ultra modern sector. But she has not made any attempt regarding the financial size of the fishermen and the role of banks towards the upliftment of their economic standards.

Mishra Ava in her study "The Socio-Economic Conditions of Chilika Fishermen—A study of their problems and prospects" (1998) deals with social matters regarding the family of fishermen, such as family size, sex, composition, age group and technology used by them. Hence she gives a review of literature of Chilika lake and development of fish marketing in Orissa during plan periods. She has suggested that socio-economic conditions of fishermen have not been reported. No development work will be fruitful unless the bene-ficiaries of the area are closely related to different schemes. She has studied the various problems of fishermen in detail and how they are being exploited by the middlemen. But she has not highlighted the financial aspect which is most important.

Mishra Rabinarayan (2005) in his article, "Development of Production of Fish in Freshwater in Orissa" has observed that fishery is a very profitable business. By using latest technology fish production can be increased up to 4000 kg per acre. Pisciculture has made a significant contribution in Orissa. In the year 2003-04 its share is 62 per cent out of whole production of fisheries. He also suggests various steps to improve the fish production. He concluded that if proper technology is used in production it will increase more than one ton per hectare and make Orissa a surplus state.

Valliammai, A and C. Thangamuthu (2004) in their article "Environmental Issue in Prawn Culture" suggested that prawn culture fetches sizeable export earnings and also supplies good nutritive food to the population. Though one cannot ignore the environmental implications, it would be economically unwise to suggest a total ban on prawn culture. Prawn fanning in India has taken a new dimension in recent years. The writer also gives a detailed account of foreign exchange earned through the export of prawns.

Sahu Anil Kumar and Sudhansu Sekhar Nayak (2005) in their article "Fishereis in Orissa: A management look" suggested that introduction of Bay of Bengal programme of small scale industries was instrumental in launching a number of programmes in the state. They also discussed the importance of ice and boat making and stressed on providing educational programme in fishing villages, and the participation of poor fishing communities in various schemes to uplift their economic conditions.

Kokate, K. D. and S. M. Upare in their article " Role of Fisheries in Rural development" state that fishery sector in India has been giving employment to 59.60 lakh full time or part time fishermen. The contribution of fishery sector to the gross domestic product of the country is approximately 1.3°. They made a study of Maharashtra which is ranked third in marine fish production in the country. An indepth study has been made about export earnings from fish and fisheries products from Maharashtra. The role of women in fisheries is also discussed and list of fishery research station and Krishi Vigyan Kendra are also provided. They also suggested that awareness on utilization of available resources is the prime need among the fishermen community and various other recommendations are also made.

Misra, R. N. (2003) in his article "Stock of Water for Fish Cultivation" observes that people have developed new technique to collect water from different sources and make a reservoir for fish cultivation made from such water. The whole technique is not to allow water to drift away towards unproductive use. During rainy season, rainwater is collected with a view to cultivate in the surroundings of paddy cultivation land and as such fishes are cultivated. In mountain ranges check dams are being constructed to preserve water where fish cultivation is made. Similarly minor irrigation resources are used for pisciculture.

Choudhry, R. P. and Mr. H. Nayak (1995) in their article "Aquaculture and its Infrastructural Development in Orissa" state that Orissa epitomises the poverty of India. Aquaculture has a vast potential for direct employment of skilled and unskilled, educated and uneducated rural people of the state. Infrastructure like land, road, electricity, water supply, technical expertise, finance should be provided. To sum up. aquaculture has tremendous potential for rural employment, social development, economic growth and export benefits to a poor State like Orissa.

Agarwal, S. C. (2003) provides basic knowledge about fish farming. There are varieties of fish in which only a few of them are culturable having specific feeding habit. The basic information about culturable varieties is essential for proper culture practice. The maintainance and management of fish pond is necessary for fish health and growth. The economic aspect of any culture system is very important and has direct bearing on the culturist.

Srivastava, C.B.L. (2004) provides a comprehensive modern account of the fishery science. It provides an in-depth study about world fisheries, Indian fisheries, fish as food commodity, fish population and different fishing gears used by fishermen. He also has the view that fish culture on commercial scale is a recent innovation to fisheries but it has assumed great significance for the better prospect it holds. Fish culture is practised in both fresh water and salt water with expanding fisheries. Fish production started influencing the national economy of the countries to a large extent.

Norman, J.P. (1963) deals with fishes and different kind of fishes. He has regarded fish not as museum specimens but as living organisms which have been modified in a multitude of ways in accordance with the nature of their surroundings and to fit them for the particular conditions under which they are compelled to live. He also deals with fishes and its cultivation by man. It also says about utility of fishes as a source of vitamin, protein and other nutritional value. He has also discussed in detail about dangers of overfishing, possible remedies for fish diseases and also fishes being used in controlling diseases.

Objective and Scope of the Study

The district of Ganjam has 3171 villages. The population of the district is 31,36,937 out of which the fishermen population stands at 93,686 as per 2001 Census. It constitutes nearly three per cent of the total population. The total fishing area of the district has a coast line of 60 km out of 3171 villages of the district fishermen villages constitute 444. Though the fishermen of the district contribute an important share in export from the district, still they are poor, illiterate, backward and live below poverty line. Keeping this in view, the study is undertaken to causes of their low economic standard. It also studies how a change is brought about in their life patterns by sufficient and timely financial help to them. The Government of Orissa has also formulated the policy for fishen development in the year 1996 and its full implementation is yet to be awaited.

It also studies the relative contribution of institutional agencies and non-institutional financial agencies for the development of economic standard of the subjects under study. It also studies the economic condition of these subjects before and after availing the finance from these financial institutions. Further, it examines how these institutions, banks have affected the rate of socio-economic development after advancing their funds. A field study is made on the basis of questionnaire administered on the sample population by visiting their houses.

1200 samples are taken adopting random sample methods for this purpose of the study. The present study being a fact finding research aims at investigating the magnitude of the problem regarding the use of the fund for economic development of the fishermen. It also studies the misuse of the fund for economic development by the fishermen of the district. It examines the bottlenecks that stand on the way of growth and development of not only the fish industries of the district, but also the economic instabilities of the fishermen.

As the study is empirical by nature it is confined to one district of the state of Orissa, the Ganjam district. The scope of the study is limited only to the fishermen who have taken loans either from financial institutions or private parties to improve the fishing industries and their comparative contribution towards it.

Period of the Study

The study has covered a period of eleven years from 1995-96 to 2005-06. Longer period could not be taken into account for the fear of lengthy and elaborate analysis of the data collected as well as undue expansion of the size of the study.

Hypotheses

The study aims at testing a set of hypotheses after careful evaluation of the findings. Keeping in view the objectives of the study and also taking various internal and external factors for the purpose, the following hypotheses are considered after careful analysis of the data gathered from various sources. The following hypotheses are taken for due examinations either to be confirmed or rejected by taking the pros and corns of the study. The hypotheses are:

1. The RRB's are taking very important steps in financing the fishermen of the district in comparison to other banks like commercial banks and co operatives.
2. Non-marketing of fish in time creates problem for economic development of the fishermen.
3. The fishermen are not using modem techniques for catching fish and mostly use the traditional methods which create restriction for the economic development of the fishermen.
4. Non-institutional agencies play an important role in financing the fishermen in comparison to the institutional agencies.
5. The borrowers who take more loans from the institutional agencies repay within a specified time, but the number of defaulter keep on rising as the loan amount decreases.
6. As sea fishing is seasonal and fish is not available throughout the year, it hampers the economic development of the fishermen.

Collection of Data

The data for the purpose of study have been collected from two sources. They are:

Primary Source

The primary data have been collected for the following objectives:

1. To study the socio-economic condition of fishermen who have taken loan from various financial institutions.
2. To find out the style of utilization of institutional loan and non-institutional loan by the fishermen of the sample district.

3. To know the repaying behaviour of loan taken by the fishermen.
4. To find out the probable reasons for the non-utilization of loan in proper way.
5. To study the economic growth of fishermen after taking institutional loans to improve their fish culture.

Secondary Source

The data from secondary sources include published books and journals. A good deal of library work was done by visiting various Universities of the state, state libraries, district libraries. For the purpose of collection of data various libraries outside the state are also visited and information is collected for the purpose of the study. Further, various journals, committee reports, survey reports, bulletins, newspapers, various statistical journals are used for up-to-date secondary data in theoretical chapters.

Sampling Design

The sampling design is made by considering the objectives and scope of the study. It has been decided to choose the beneficiaries on the basis of representation sampling. The sampling district Ganjam has the population of 31,36,937 lakh as per 2001 Census. Thus a sample of 1200 has been taken by using random sampling methods for the purpose of the study.

Method of Analysis

Analysis has been divided into three parts.

The first part of the analysis is on the socio-economic condition of the fishermen of the sample district of Ganjam. The second part of the study being covered in Chapter 4 is on the role of different banks in financing the fishermen and has analysed the sources of institutional loan and non-institutional loan from different sources and their utilization.

The third part of the study being covered in (Chapter 6) deals with the collected data which have been analysed to find out the proper use of the institutional finance and non-institutional finance. It also covers non-utilization of funds and the socio economic development of fishermen after utilization of loans. In this chapter the hypotheses selected in chapter one dealing with Introduction and methodology are tested and some conclusions are derived after through examination of the study. This part of analysis has been exhaustively dealt with in Chapter 7.

Tool of Analysis

Various statistical tools like percentages, averages, ratios have been used at different levels for analysis of the collected data. A number of study illustrative, significant and clear.

Thus it becomes necessary to present the collected data in the thesis in the form of tables, diagrams, photos, annexure etc to make the study clear.

Limitations of the Study

Ganjam district in the state of Orissa has been selected as sample district for the purpose of the study due to limitation of time and resources. Further, the period of study was confined from 1995-96 to 2005-06 to study the behavioural activities of the loanee on repayment and the use of institutional loans of the borrowings. 1200 beneficiaries have been selected at random from the sample district. Hence all the limitations of random sampling methods are focused in the study covering 10 years.

The primary data are collected by a designed Questionnaire as per the information provided by the beneficiaries of the sample district. It can not be considered as hundred per cent accurate. The primary data also has its own limitations.

The problem of financing institutions providing loans to the fishermen of the sample district are not taken into consideration for the purpose of our study. So it has its own limitations.

Hundred per cent accuracy cannot be attached to the secondary data collected from different sources which are used in the study.

The data of the secondary nature has its own limitation. For the purpose of analysis, various statistical tools have been used and they have their own limitations.

Chapter

2

Socio-Economic Profile of Fishermen

Introduction

India is vast country, covered by water on three sides and land on one. The Arabian sea, the Bay of Bengal and Indian Ocean provide the subcontinent with plenty of marine fish. India too have large number of small and big rivers which provide immense variety and quality of fresh water fish. In the field of fishery, India ranks seventh in the world scenario, covering an area of 3.29 million sq. km of coastline, holding a share of 25 per cent of the world's total of 133.29 million sq.km of coast area. The main land extends between latitudes 84°N′ and 37° 6′ N and longitude 68° 7′ E and 97° 25′ E and measures about 327 km from north to south between the extreme latitudes and about 2933 km from East to West between the extreme longitudes. It has a land frontier of 15,200 km and a coastline of 8085 kms including mainland, Lakshadweep, Andaman and Nicobar islands. The country possesses more than 1000 million human population at present, which accounts for over 15 per cent of the global population. It is growing at an annual rate of over 2 per cent, thus adding 16-18 million every year, playing an important role in Asian fisheries and aquaculture scenario. India produces over 2.44 mt from the inland fishery sector, and occupies second position in the world.

India has an enormous potential resources teeming with fish. A large part of the country is maritime, engaged in traditional fishing in marine water from ages. The inland fishing is also an age old practice in the extensive network of fresh waters. India is witnessing a sea change in its activities on the fisheries horizon. Marine fish production levels started plateauing and catches from inland waters are getting subjected to limitation due to construction of dams, barrages on river course and increasing pollution hazards. Contrary to this, aquaculture which used to be just a means of earnings livelihood for rural poor, till recently, has now emerged as a coveted business for one and all. It has started receiving increasing investment from all quarters and has assumed the status of an industry. On the contrary, however, brackish water aquaculture of late has been facing some problems, like shrimp disease, ill-formed apprehension of its adverse impact on the environment and a number of ill-conceived litigation.

The changing scenario has now necessitated handling of fisheries and aquaculture programmes of the country with a greater degree of depth and precision. Newer methods are required to be explored for obtaining greater levels of fish production for meeting protein requirements of the expanding population. For this living near the shore waters where the fish catches has already touched maximum sustainable yield (m/y) level. Resources of the off shore water and deep sea will have to be tapped. Productivity of inland water has to be raised through ranching programmes and popularizing the systems of aquaculture in cages and pens. Likewise solutions to a host of associated problems (disease outbreak, possible environmental degradation, disturbance in the socio-economic fisher folk etc.), are emerging due to sudden upsurge of aquaculture. Industry will also have to be tackled. All these reveal the increasing complexities of the growing fishes, and aquaculture activities in the country. This calls for a totally redesigned and revitalized form of fisheries education and attentions in India.

The future of blue-revolution in India lies in raising the productivity over marine brackish water sector. India's population is increasing at a very fast rate. Demand for fish is bound to increase in the coming years and at present level of Gross Domestic Product (GDP), it is estimated around 9.50 million tons. It means the country has to almost double its fish production by AD 2020. It is hoped that full potential of the fisheries resources can be realized not only on the basis of technologies developed, but also the technologies disseminated.

There is no short cut to development. No general rule of thumbs would work for sustainable aquaculture. The four pillars of development—such as research, education, extension and training must get equal support and treatment. To bring objectivity, workability and professionalism in extension, all these elements must work in proper harmony and relationship.

Considering the prevalent production levels in ponds and tanks in different states of the country with due reference to the agro ecological conditions, fish species, technology adoption levels, demand pattern, export potentials, and predicted growth in freshwater aquaculture sector in different states should catch our imagination. A strategic plan for augmenting fish production from fresh water aquaculture operation in Aqua Gold (Matsyavandar) is proposed. It promises fish production to 3.31 mt from fresh water sector alone on implementation over a period of 5 year plan. Such achievements need a meticulously, diligent strategic plan.

With a coastline of over 8,118 km. and an Exclusive Economic zone of over 2 mn sq. km, India has a significant marine fisheries sector that has long been an important source of occupation and livelihood for the coastal communities of the country. It is estimated that at least 3 million people derive their livelihood from marine capture fisheries. There are 3,600 fishing villages situated along the Indian Coastline. Other estimates put the number of people dependent on marine fisheries as much higher. The majority of these in the sector are small scale and artisanal processing and small scale trading activities. Fishermen statistics of India is depicted in Table 2.1

Table 2.1 reveals the fishermen statistics of India relating to marine fisheries. Table also shows the marine fishermen population, household along with, marine villages and fish landing centres.

Table 2.1. Fishermen Statistics of India

Marine fishermen population	3 mm
Marine fishermen households	0.50 mm
No. of active fishermen	1.025 mn
Marine fishing villages	3,638
Fish landing centres	2,251

Source: Central Marine Fisheries Research Institute, Coachin, p.1.

The Fishery Resources

The fishery resources are broadly divided into two classes.

(*i*) Inland fisheries and

(*ii*) Marine fisheries.

Inland Fisheries

The inland fisheries are a heterogeneous class, which covers culture fisheries that is fishing in ponds, natural and artificial lakes, swamps, rivers and canals. Apart from these, fishing in coastal lagoon, estuaries and creeks has now become a part of inland fisheries, as both brackish water and fresh water aquaculture are included in this class. India is rank second in the world in inland fish production. A glimpse of India's diversified inland resources is shown in Table 2.2.

Table 2.2 provides a glimpse of inland fishery resources of India. It shows river, mangroves, estuaries, reserves and upland lakes.

Marine Fisheries

This is wholly a capture-oriented sector and is largely exploited by marine fishermen through traditional and mechanized crafts and gears.

Table 2.2. Fishery Resources of India

Resources	Resources Size
River (km)	29,000
Mangroves (ha)	3,56,000
Estuaries (ha)	3,00,000
Estuarine wetland (ha)	39,000
Backwater/Lagoon (ha)	1,90,500
Large and medium reservoirs (ha)	16,67,809
Small reservoir (ha)	4,485,557
Flood plan wetland (ha)	2,02,313
Upland Lakes (ha)	7,20,000

Source: Central Marine Fisheries Research Institute, Coachin p.1.

More than 70 per cent of the fish landings in India are from the West coast and the rest from the East coast. The marine fishery resources are broadly divided into (1) Demersal and (2) Pelagic Resources. The Demersal resources includes Sharks and Rays; Eels, perches, red mullets, polynemid, scianeids. Soles and other miscellaneous species. Crustaceans, which are shellfish like prawn, non-penaeid prawn, lobsters, crabs etc. have included in demersal resources, inese are usuany luuuu 500 m depth and taken together their maximum sustainable yield is 84,000 metric tonnes per year.

The pelagic resources are usually telubed with the mid-water resources and it include oil, sardines, Hilsa, Ilisha, Clupeids, Flying fish, Mackeral, Tunnies, Catfish, Achavilla, Bombay Duck, Ribbon fish, Mugil, Saurees, Pomprets and other Cephalopods. These resources can be exploited lower to 100 metres depth zone and their maximum sustainable yield is 40,800 metric tonnes per year (Lawson, 1984).

The marine fishing sector in all the coastal State of India can be divided into three sub-sectors. These are as follows:

1. Traditional sector : It involves off–shore fishing operation with non-mechanised boats and traditional gears and operate within the 16 km to 20km range from the coastline.

2. Modern sector : This sector with its small mechanized crafts and traditional crafts operate within the mid sea, area within the 200km range from the shore.

3. Ultra modern sector : This sector with its large vessels namely deep-sea trawlers operate in the deep-sea zone and beyond the operational area of the former two sub-sectors.

Indian Exclusive Economic Zone

The 2.02 millon square km water spreads in an area of the Exclusive Economic Zone. In India, it extends up to 200 nautical miles with 8,085 km of coastline of the country from west to east around the peninsular India. The maritime States are Gujurat, Maharashtra, Goa, Karnataka, Kerala, Tamil Nadu, Lakshadweep, Pondicherry, Andhra Pradesh, Orissa, West Bengal and Andaman and Nicobar islands. It is illustrated in Table 2.3.

Table 2.3. Potential of Fishery Resources in the Indian Exclusive Economic Zone

Depth Range (m)	0-50	50-200	200-500	Oceanic	Total
Demersal	1.28	0.625	0.03	0.00	1.933
Neretic Pelagic	1.00	0.74	0.00	0.00	1.74
Oceanic Pelagic	0.00	0.00	0.00	0.25	0.246
Total	**2.28**	**1.369**	**0.028**	**0.246**	**3.921**
Percentage	58.1	34.9	0.07	6.3	100

Source: Handbook of Fishery Statistics, 2000-01, Government of Orissa, p. 10.

Table 2.3 shows total depth range relating to demersal. Neretic Pelagic, and oceanic pelagic and also shows total and percentage of catch.

Production of Fish in India

India is one of the major fish producing countries. Table 2.4 shows the production of fish by different States.

Table 2.4. Production of Fish in India (in 1,000 mt)

Sl. No.	States/Union Territories	2000-01	2001-02	2002-03	2003-04
1	2	3	4	5	6
1.	Andhra Pradesh	589.69	676.11	827.90	944.64
2.	Arunachal Pradesh	2.50	2.60	2.60	2.65
3.	Assam	158.62	161.45	165.52	181.00
4.	Bihar	222.16	240.40	261.00	266.49
5.	Goa	71.57	69.92	76.53	87.36
6.	Gujarat	660.74	701.60	777.90	654.62
7.	Haryana	33.04	34.57	35.18	39.13
8.	Himachal Pradesh	7.02	7.22	7.24	6.53
9.	Jammu & Kashmir	17.51	18.85	19.75	19.75
10.	Karnataka	303.37	249.61	266.42	257.00
11.	Kerala	651 .80	671.82	678.32	684.70
12.	Madhya Pradesh	48.84	47.46	42.17	50.82
13.	Maharastra	526.10	537.05	514.10	545.13
14.	Manipur	16.05	16.45	16.60	17.60
15.	Meghalaya	6.18	4.97	5.37	5.15
16.	Mizoram	2.86	3.15	3.25	3.38
17.	Nagaland	5.50	5.20	5.50	5.56
18.	Orissa	259.64	281 .95	287.53	306.95
19.	Punjab	52.00	58.00	66.00	83.65
20.	Rajasthan	12.12	14.27	25.60	14.30
21.	Sikkim	0.14	0.14	0.14	0.14
22.	Tamil Nadu	481.42	485.00	473.50	474.14
23.	Tripura	29.42	29.45	29.52	17.98
24.	Uttar pradesh	208.29	225.37	249.84	267.00
25.	West Bengal	1060.23	1100.10	1120.00	1169.60
26.	A & N Island	27.69	27.08	28.30	31.15

1	2	3	4	5	6
27.	Chandigarh	0.08	0.04	0.08	0.08
28.	D & N Haveli	0.04	0.06	0.05	0.05
29.	Daman & Diu	16.38	21.52	11.26	13.77
30.	Delhi	3.98	3.20	2.25	2.10
31.	Lakshadweep	12.00	13.65	7.50	10.0.3
32.	Pondicherry	43.30	44.50	45.02	48.00
33.	Chhatisgarh	43.39	95.76	99.80	111.05
34.	Uttarankhand	9.07	6.42	2.55	2.56
35.	Jharkhanda	42.60	101.00	45.38	75.38
	India	5625.34	5955.94	6199.68	6399.44

Source: Economic survey, Government of Orissa, 2005-06, Annexure. 29.

Table 2.4 clearly indicates the fact that production of fish in India is constantly increasing since 2000-01. The largest share comes from West Bengal followed by Gujurat and Kerala. The top three States contribute annually 50 per cent of the total production. Currently India occupies tenth position in world fisheries.

Marine Fishery Resources

Table 2.5 will show the State with the approximate length of coast with number of landing centre and fishing villages.

Table 2.5 clearly shows the length of the coastline, continental shelf area, and no. of landings etc. of different States of India. Gujurat has longest coast line of 1600km. Andaman & Nicobar Islands have a coastline of only 27 km, having seven landing centre and 31 villages.

Fish Productions

The major fish producing countries with their inland and marine fish production is depicted in Table 2.6.

Table 2.5. Marine Fishery Resource-coastal States and Union Territories

States/UTs	Approx. length of coastline (in km)	Continental self (1000 sq. km)	No. of landing centres	No. of fishing villages
Andhra Pradesh	974	33	508	508
Goa	104	10	88	72
Gujarat	300	27	29	221
Karnataka	1600	184	286	851
Kerala	590	40	226	395
Maharashtra	720	112	184	329
Orissa	480	24	63	556
Tamil Nadu	1076	41	362	652
West Bengal	158	17	47	45
A & N islands	1912	35	57	31
Daman & Diu	27	0	7	10
Lakhadweep	132	4	11	45
Pondicherry	45	1	28	
Total	8118	528	1896	3937

Source: Economic Survey, Government of Orissa 2000-01, p. 109

Table 2.6. Fish Production of Major Fish Producing Countries 2004 (in '000 MT)

Sl. No.	Country	Inland	Marine	Total
1.	China	16820	24748	411568
2.	Peru	33	10625	10658
3.	Japan	83	5669	5752
4.	Chile	00	4692	4692
5.	U.S.A.	311	4863	5174
6.	Russian Federation	358	3690	4048
7.	Indonesia	734	4195	4928
8.	Norway	01	3191	3191
9.	Rep. of Korea	15	2132	2146
10.	India	2838	2852	5689
	Total	28,602	101,831	130,433

Source: Economic Survey, Government of Orissa, 2005-06, Anx. -30

Table 2.6 indicates that China holds the first position followed by Peru and Japan. It also shows that marine fish catch accounts for a greater percentage to inland fisheries. Hence marine fishing has become more popular through out the world. Total marine catch is higher than inland fishing.

Marine Fish Production

India's marine fish production has increased more than five times, from 0.53 tonnes in 1950-51 to 2.81 tonnes in 2000-01, to 2852 mt in 2004-05. Approximately is from mechanized fishing units causing trawls, gillnets and purse-seines), while the rest is from motorized fishing units (using gillnets, gears and purse-seines with cut board motors) and form empowered fishing units. Available reports indicate that fisheries in several parts of the country are under stress with most of the major commercially exploited stocks showing signs of over exploitation. This has repercussions on the livelihood, of those dependent on these resources, and better management of resources is clearly called. Table 2.7 shows the production of fish in India.

Table 2.7. Fish Production of India

(Quality in '000 mt)

Year	Production (in mt)
2000-01	5625.34
2001-02	5955.94
2002-03	6169.77
2003-04	6399.04

Source: Economic Survey, Government of Orissa, 2005-06. Anx. 29.

Table 2.7 shows the increase in fish production of India from the year 2000-2001 to 2003-04. It was 5625.34 mt in 2000-01 but increased to 6399.44 mt in 2003-04.

Marine water offers lucrative fishing which include the Arabian sea, the Bay of Bengal, a number of bays, gulfs, back waters, lagoons, coral reefs, tidal estuaries, swamps etc.

Bio-geographical Zones

Fishing is generally limited to 11 to 16 km wide coastal waters having a total continental shelf area of 2,59,000 sq. km along the 5650 km long coastline. Twelve biogeographical zones are distinguished along the coastline. They are:

1. Kerala and South Malabar
2. Malabar and South Kanara
3. Konkan
4. Mumbai and Gujurat
5. Kathiawar
6. Palk bay and Gulf of Mannar
7. Coromondal South
8. Coromandal North
9. Andhra South
10. Andhra Middle
11. Andhra North
12. West Bengal and Orissa.

Important fishing areas on the west coast includes: Gujarat Areas, Konkan area, North Canara area, South Canara area and Malabar area.

On the East Coast

It consist the Gulf of Mannar area, Coromondal area, Telugu area and Delta area. There are about 1200 landing centres on the coastline. The west coast is much more productive than the east coast. About 75 per cent of the total landing comes from the west coast. The great single species fisheries such as the Sardine fishery, the mackenel fishery, the prawn fishery are confined to the west coast.

Ocean character of the Arabian Sea chiefly accounts for the striking difference in the productivity of the west coast and the east coast. Oceanic currents influenced for the Bottom Antarctic drift and the Somali, which come from the East coast of Africa and finally move along the west coast of India. South west monsoon coupled with North-westernly wind and the ocean currents cause upwelling along the west coast a thorough circulation in coastal waters which help in rise of nutrient rich deep waters to the surface upwelling also helps in the circulation.

The upwelling starts first in the northern coastal waters. Its intensity is maximum at Calicut and at Mangalore. During the peak period of monsoon temperature discontinuity appears at a depth of 20 metre whereas oxygen discontinuity layers move to surface and these are necessary antecedents for upwelling. By December, sinking of surface water beings produces eventually isothermal layers. A number of eddy formations about Calicut also contribute to making of surface and deep waters. All these contribute immensely to the fertility of the waters in the production of flora. Planktons production is amazingly large throughout the coastal waters of the west coast. Malabar coast is especially rich in plankton between Alleppy and north of Calicut where long mud banks occur in sub-surface water. Mud banks are fine silt particles setting along the coast, highly rich in phosphates and other nutrients that help in the production of plankton. The catch composition of the fisheries along the west coast shows regional variations. However, pomfrets, polynemids, and prawns occur along the entire west coast. Kathiwar coast has important fisheries of scianids, polynemids, clupeids, sharks and Rays. Gujurat coast supports the Bombay duck fishery. Bombay coast, Konkan coast and the Malabar Coast have the major fisheries of the sardines, mackerels, anchovies, soles, sharks and rays. Fishing is intense during September to February, low in March and insignificant during June to August (the period of monsoon). The east coast, on the other hand, does not support any single commercially large fisheries but several small fisheries.

The availability of fish varies which includes clupeids and cat fishes in north-east coast; Trichirus, Pellona, Silver bellies, Sharks in Andhra coast; silver bellies, seers, flying fishes, Sharks and rays in Coromondal coast; Lactanius,

Hamiramphus, Silver bellies and Pomfrets in Tuticorin and Gulf of Mannar.

India is holding 10th position among the fish producing countries of the world. Although India possesses good marine resource, her production is only 3 per cent of the total world's fish production. This may be due to the reason that a large area of the sea is yet to be exploited and also due to primitive methods of fishing adopted for catching fish. India has total coastline of 8,129 km including Andaman and Nicobar islands and Lakshadweep island. India has nine marine States and four union territories. The States are Gujarat, Maharashtra, Goa, Karnataka, Kerala, Tamil Nadu, Andhra Pradesh, Orissa and West Bengal.

Now-a-days fish production is not much significant with a vast area in the economic zone in East and west coast of India. It is possible to produce an additional catch up 10-25 million tonnes. After the declaration of EEZ by India, the country has nearly 2.02 million sq. km for exploitation. The west coast is producing 72 per cent of fish while east coast is producing only 28 per cent. In the east coast the average width of continental shelf is 32-40 km while in west coast it is 64-160 km miles being maximum at Mumbai coast. The total fish production from Marine & Inland source is 5.38 mt. This is illusrated in Table 2.8.

Table 2.8 shows that among all the maritime States of India, Gujarat plays the first position followed by Andhra Pradesh, Tamil Nadu, Kerala, Maharashtra and West Bengal. But now-a-days the maximum contribution of capture fishes are 60-70 per cent by mechanised boats and 25-30 per cent by traditional boats. The present level of exploitation of marine resources is about 75 per cent of the estimated potential of the EEZ. It was only 60 per cent in 1995-96. About 60-70 per cent of the marine catch comes from west coast and 25-35 per cent from east-coast and about 5 per cent from the islands. Pelagic fishes contributes 40-60 per cent, Dermersal fishes contributes about 35-45 per cent, Crustaceans contributes 15-20 per cent. Moluscans includes chank fisheries in the range of 5-15 per cent.

North-west Coast

North west coast composes Gujarat and Maharashtra, which contributes about 5-8 lakh tonnes of marine catch. The demersal fishes dominant with more than 60 per cent of the catch. Since the continental shelf is the most important species of demersal group is the Mumbai Duck. Other important group of fishes are scianid, pompfrt, sharks, ray, cat fishes. Among the pelagic fishes clupeids like Hilsa is dominated while ribbon fishes contributed subsequently in the crustaceans groups. The non-penaeids, are most important while penaeids are landed in significant quantity.

Table 2.8. Maritime States, coast line and continental shelf

Sl. No.	State UTs	Coast line (km)	Coast line (%)	Continental shelf (sq. km.)	Continental shelf (%)
01.	Gujurat	1500	26.5	120000	27.4
02.	A.P	980	17.3	39109	7.9
03.	Tamil Nadu & Pondichery	960	17	34820+2488	8.5
04.	West Bengal & Orissa	200 + 480 = 680	12	7094+ 120166	8.5
05.	Maharashtra	600	10.6	—	—
06.	Kerala	560	9.9	38073	8.8
07.	Karnataka	270	4.8	24999	5.7
08.	Goa	110	1.9	9809	2.2
09.	A & N Lakshadweep	—	—	34965 7770	1.8

Source : A Textbook of Fishery Science and Indian Fisheries, p. 34.

South-west Coast

Along the south-west coast Goa, Karnatak, Kerala contribute about 5-8 lakhs tonnes of fishe. The pelagic harvests are heavily dependant as oil sardine and makerel stocks. The other important stocks are sardine, ribbon fishes, white baits, carangids, tunnies, sheer fishes, silver bellies and flat fishes. The peneids are most important and highly valuable.

South-East Coast

The south east coast represents Tamil Nadu, Pondicherry and Andhra Pradesh. It's contribution is about 3-4 lakhs tonnes of catch. Almost equal quantity of pelagic and demersal fishes are caught. In pelagic groups lesser sardines, other clupeids, ribbonfishes, carangids, mackerels and ship fishes are important. In the demersal group silver bellies form about 20 per cent followed by elasmobranch, cat fishes, scianids. Among crustaceans, penaeid, shrimp lobster, crabs are important.

North-East Coast

The Orissa and West Bengal are poorly exploited. Annual landing is about 1-2 lakhs tonnes with equal quantity of pelagic and demersal group. The clupids are important group with hilsa contribute a large share of pelagic landing. In the later categories Mumbai duck, Scianids, catfishes, porn frets are important. Among crustacean penaeids, shrimps contribute the major share. In general the composition of catches resemble to west coast.

Inland Capture Fishries

Inland capture fisheries of India contributes to 30 per cent of the total fish production. The large network of inland water masses will continue to provide great potential for economic capture fishery which consequently will compete well with fast growing fish culture practices. The fresh water inland water bodies fall into five major categories, distinguished as the Ganga, the Bramhaputra and the Indus system of the northern India and the east and west coast river system of the southern India. The river system has certain characteristics of their own with respect to their ecology, climatic conditions and fish populations of commercial food fishes. Besides, there are a number of land locked lakes. Especially these are situated at high altitudes which has started supporting cold water fisheries of both indigenous and exotic species. In addition to the above-mentioned freshwaters, there are also rich fisheries offered by extensive brackish waters including important estuaries (Hoogly, Matlah, Mahanadi and Godavari estuaries), Lagoon (Chilika lake, Pulicat lake), and back waters (Vembanad) and paddy field (Pokkali in Kerala). Chilika lake, in the State of Orissa is an open shallow brackish water lake having an area about 906 sq. km in summer and 1165 sq. km, in rainy season. A long canal joins it with sea. Water from river Daya (Mahanadi) and other smaller streams flow into it. Recent, additions to the natural inland water bodies are man made reservoirs. There are at present some 300 reservoirs, which hold very good prospects for restocking, both for capture as well as culture fisheries. Some of these reservoirs have responded fairly well to attempts to restock them with indigenous as well as exotic species.

Inland capture fisheries is a continually expanding industry bringing under its fold newer fisheries of a local or regional nature. In order to improve the existing fisheries, introduction of exotic species from abroad and inter regional transplantation of fish from northern to southern water have become most productive and profitable.

The inland capture fishery, however, stands at a critical juncture which draws a special attention at the national level. Rapid industrialization movement in the country have given a serious blow to the growth of the inland fisheries which was struggling to come out of the old fashioned style to a more rational and scientific style. Construction of dams has been the cause of decline and damage to several regionally important fisheries. Industrial discharge coupled with mushrooming growth of inland water bodies are polluting water in large proportions and damaging the fish population tremendously. Indiscriminate fishing of fingerlings and juveniles, which support local and seasonal fisheries in breeding or nursery grounds have been doing enormous damage and effective control are needed for conservation. Likewise time old practice of sewage disposal into rivers was a menacing practice causing heavy pollution. Great harm is also being done from agricultural practice causing heavy pollution as agricultural wash coming to inland water, which brings to fish a very toxic principle of the numerous pesticides used in the agricultural practices.

Reservoir Fisheries

Over 800 reservoirs scattered over various river system are recent additions to fish resources. The great water mass they hold is being exploited for developing a number of local fisheries as well as of exotic species. These include Indian major carps in the northern reservoirs and peninsular carps in the southern India.

Inter-generic hybrids are occurring spontaneously in reservoir. Reservoir conditions open new hopes and thought to favour natural hybridization, because as compared to reverine conditions, reservoirs, owing to dam formation, create scarcity of certain species and preponderance of others. Under these conditions, inter generic breeding is promoted. Catla-rohu hybrid occurring naturally in Rihand reservoir and in Rangwan reservoir in up is one good example that has recently came into light. The hybrid is more suitably adapted to reservoir then its parent Rohu which is poorly adopted to large scale water level fluctuations and to the eco-system of reservoirs. The hybrid combines all the good feature of Rohu and Catla and is also giving indications of attaining sexual maturity, thus opening hopes for sustained population.

Reservoirs of India

There are different reservoirs which is depicted in Table 2.9.

Table 2.9 shows different dams located in different states and their related rivers. At present there are 20 dams and the highest number belongs to Uttar Pradsh. Reservoir fishery has attracted attention only recently, whereas the reservoirs hold great production potential ecologically. Lack of proper management is generally the cause of low average food fish production i.e. 10 kg/ha/year. Efforts are currently a foot to plan higher yields on the basis of management, which is ecology-oriented. On the other hand, it guarantees assured supply of fish seed for massive restocking and other measures of control. Gill nets are the only gears used at present in the deep waters of reservoirs.

Table 2.9. Important Reservoirs of India

Sl. No.	Name of Dam	State	River
1.	Rihand	Uttar Pradesh	Ganga
2.	Dhandraul	Uttar Pradesh	Bhakarr
3.	Sard Sagar	Uttar Pradesh	Chuka Sanda (Ganga)
4.	Dhora	Uttar Pradesh	Dhora
5.	Mutatila	Uttar Pradesh	Ganga
6.	Govind Sagar	Punjab & Himachal Pradesh	Sutlej
7.	Beas	Punjab & H.P.	Beas
8.	Hirakud	Orissa	Mahanadi
9.	Rana Pratap Sagar	Rajasthan	Barakar (Ganga)
10.	Mainthan	Bihar	Barakar (Ganga)
11.	Panchet	Bihar	Damodar (Ganga)
12.	Gandhi Sagar	Madhya Pradesh	Chambal (Ganga)
13.	Mettur	Tamil Nadu	Cauvery
14.	Bhavani Sagar	Tamil Nadu	Bhavani
15.	Nagarjun Sagar	Andhra Pradesh	Krishna
16.	Niam Sagar	Andhra Pradesh	Mowgina
17.	Tunngabhadra	Karnataka	Tungabhadra
18.	Krishnanat Sagar	Karnataka	(Krisha)
19.	Neyyar	Kerala	Cauvery
20.	Ukaj	Gujarat	Neyyar

Source : A Text Book of Science and Fishery Science of Indian Fisheries, p. 28.

Cold Water Fisheries

Cold water fisheries have a great scope in the upland water masses of India which are significantly abundant in the Himalayan regions of Kashmir, Himanchal Pradesh, Uttarakhand, Meghalaya, North Bengal, Sikkim, Bhutan and Arunachal Pradesh and in the Deccan plateau region of the peninsular part of the country viz. Tamil Nadu and Kerala. These water bodies have cold water that can sustain only the so-called cold-water fishes, and hence have a fishery different from that of the plains. The upland water comprises of hill streams with rapids and pools, lakes of all the three kinds eutrophic, oligotropic and mesotrophic and man-made reservoirs with high dams. Whereas the hill streams are rain-fed in the Deccan plateau of the South. These are fed, in addition by the melting snow of high altitudes or from springs coming down the slope.

In the northern some of the lakes, viz. Vishensar, Shishnag, Neel Nag, etc. of Kashmir, which completely freeze during the winter, others only go colder of the reservoirs. Some are relatively more of standing water and non-flowing type than others. Development of fisheries is therefore restricted to the cold water species. These fishes have a good low temperature tolerance. The lower level which is in the range of 0°C to 4°C and the upper level in the range of 22° C to 30°C. Commercially, important species include exotic trout, the brown tract, *Salmo trulta fario*, the rainbow trout, *Salmo gairdneri*. The former supporting the highly paying sport-fishing in Kashmir, Himanchal Pradesh, Uttar Pradesh and the latter in the Tamil Nadu and Kerala. Sport fishing is also significantly contributed by the indigenous Mahaseer in Himachal Pradesh, Kashmir, Uttarakhand and Kerala. Capture fishery, regional or local, does not attain commercial importance except of course in the case of indigeneous snow tract (a carp) *schizothorax* spi. in Kashmir and other Himalayan streams. Some capture fishery of commercial significance also occurs in the Govindsagar Reservoir in Himachal Pradesh. Lakes and reservoirs in the uplands of the Himalayas, the Nilgins and the Manaar ranges offers lucrative culture fishery for the exotic carps. Culture of trout is an age old practice. There are trout hatcheries established in Kashmir (Harwan), in Nilgiris (Avalanche) and in Kerala (Eravikolam, Rajanallay) which are potent sources for transplantation or for restocking of streams, lakes and reservoirs of the uplands in the north and south of the country. It is from the trout hatchery at Harwan (Kashmir) that the exotic brown trout has been transplanted into the various upland waters of Kashmir, Jammu, Kulu, Kangra, Simla, Nainital, Shillong and Arunachal Pradesh. Likewise the transplantation of rainbow trout in different streams of Nilgiris was also done from fish brought from Harwan hatchery. On the other hand the reservoirs and lakes of Kerala are stocked with rainbow trout brought from Rajamallar hatchery and streams of Manaar high range from the Eravikolam hatchery.

Cold Water Lakes

There are different cold water lakes in the country which are shown in Table 2.10.

Table 2.10. Important Cold Water Lakes

Name	State
Wulur	Kashmir
Dal	Kashmir
Kishenar	Kashmir
Renuka	Himachal Pradesh
Bhimtal	Uttarakhand
Nainital	Uttarakhand
Devariatal	Uttarakhand
Sattal	Uttarakhand
Oory	Tamil Nadu
Shevanay	Tamil Nadu
Kodai Kanal	Tamil Nadu
Devicolam	Kerala
Elephant	Kerala

Source: A Text Book of Fishery Science and Indian Fisheries p. 2.19.

Table 2.10 shows important cold water lakes and the states in which they are situated. At present there are 13 cold water lakes spread over in five States.

Fisheries of the Island

The Lakshadweep yields about 10,000-16,000 tonnes of which nearly 600 tonnes are accounted as tuna. The other fishes caught in the region is elasmobranches, white baits, perches, red mullets, flying fishes, seer fish, cephalopods. From Andaman and Nicobar Islands about 10-000-15000 tonnes of fishes are landed. The important fishes are perches, ribbonfishes, mackerel and sardine.

The Indian EEZ (Exclusive Economic Zone)

The Indian EEZ came into force through the 41st Amendment to the Article 298 of the constitution. The Indian Exclusive Economic Zone surrounding the peninsula and the islands (6000 km coastline) has an area of 2.20 million square kilometre. However, only inshore water (up to 50 m depth) is actually exploited presently while the offshore water (beyond the 50 m depth) is largely unexploited. The present production of inshore water is 1.5 million tonnes per year accounting for 90 per cent of the total coastal production. The offshore water production is only 0.2 million tonnes per year which is only 40 per cent of the total production. The exploited inshore and offshore water comprise a zone within the 20 miles only (i.e. 12-14 nautical miles) 1 mile = 5280 ft., 1 nautical mile = 6076 ft or 1852 meters. The present catch of 23 million tons is just 70 per cent of the estimated potential of 3.9 million tonnes. This is because fishing is mostly confined to a depth of 50 metres. Beyond this depth the deep sea is negligibly exploited for lack of infrastructure. Deep sea fishing is holding great scope and is therefore a matter of immediate concern and attention. It is shown in Table 2.11.

Table 2.11 shows that the EEZ is almost two/thirds of the inland area of the country. It is clear that offshore is most untapped. The estimated total potential of the EEZ is from 3.9 millions tonnes to 4.5 million tonne.

Table 2.11. Indian Exclusive Economic Zone

Sub. Zone of EEZ	Annual production in million tonnes	
	Present yield	Estimated potential
(*a*) Distancewise		
Inshore up to 50 metre	1.5	2.2
Offshore beyond 50 m	0.8	2.3
Total	**2.3**	**4.5**
(*b*) Depthwise	—	—
Up to 40 fathoms	—	2.6
Between 40 & 1 00 fathoms	—	1.4
Beyond 1 00 fathoms	—	0.5
Total		**4.5**

Source : A Text Book of Fishery Science and Indian Fisheries, p. 36.

The species composition of the potential resources of the EEZ include the tuna, anchovies, perches, ribon fish, lizard fish, cat fish, shark, prawns, shrimps, lobsters. Crabs of these shrimps are the most exploited to the extent of over fishing, while tuna, squid, cattle fish and lobsters are the most untapped.

The fact that EEZ resources to the tune of about three million tonnes per year remain unexploited has been the basis for planning strategies for exploration and exploitation of the EEZ resources. Particularly in two counts viz. harvesting facilities and market (domestic and export) development.

Export Performance of Marine Products during 2005-06

The over All export of marine products has reached an All time record of 1.6 billion US$ during the year 2005-2006. The total exports aggregated to 512164 mt valued at Rs. 7245.30 crores and US$ 1644.21 million against 4613.29 mt valued at Rs. 6646.69 crores and US$ 1478.48 million during the same period of past year. The export had shown an increase of 11.02 per cent in quantity, 9.01 per cent in rupee value and 11.21 per cent realization. The unit value also increased from US$ 3.20 to US$ 3.21 per cent per kg. The details of export during the past 5 year are given in Table 2.12.

Table 2.12. Export of Marine Products of India during the Year 2005-06

Year		Export	Variation	(%)	U.V.
2001-02	Q	424470	–166003	–3.63	—
	V	5957.05	–486.84	–7.56	140.36
	$	1253.35	–16297	–11.51	2.95
2002-03	Q	467297	+42827	+10.09	—
	V	6881.31	+924.26	+ 15.52	147.26
	$	1424.90	+171.55	+13.69	3.05
2003-04	Q	412017	-55280	–11.83	—
	V	6091.95	-789.36	–11.47	147.86
	$	1330.76	-94.14	–6.61	3.23
	V	6646.69	554.74	9.11	144.09
	$	1478.48	147.71	11.10	3.20
2005-06	Q	512164	50835	11.02	—
	V	7245.03	598.61	9.01	141.46
	$	1644.21	165.74	11.21	3.21

Source : Marine product export development agency Coachin 2006.
Q = Quantity. V = Value. $ = US Dollar.

Major Items

Frozen shrimp continued to be the largest item exported in terms of value with 59.02 per cent of the total value of export and Frozen Fish continued to be the major item exported in terms of quantity with 35.60 per cent of the total volume of marine products exported from the country. The export of Frozen Shrimp was increased to the turn of 5.14 per cent, 1.20 per cent and 3.41 per cent in terms of quantity, value and US$ realization. However, the unit value has shown a short fall of 1.64 per cent in terms of USS. The

USA continued to be the major market for Indian frozen shrimp with 31.90 per cent followed by European Union with 27.98 per cent, Japan with 20.25 per cent. South East with 4.64 per cent etc. There was a shortfall in the export of frozen shrimp to Japan by 7.39 per cent as compared to the previous year. Export of frozen shrimp to European Union and USA was increased by 12.18 per cent and 0.32 per cent respectively. During the year 2005-06 Frozen Shrimp was exported to 62 countries.

The export of Frozen Fish also increased by 14.18 per cent, 31.54 per cent and 17.29 per cent in terms of quantity, rupee value, US$ and unit value realization. China is the main market for our frozen fish. 57.45 per cent accounted to China, 13.65 per cent to South East Asia, 7.31 per cent to Middle East etc. Frozen fish was exported to 63 countries during the year 2005-06.

The export of frozen cuttlefish also showed a positive growth of 12.23 per cent in quantity, 15.85 per cent in value and 18.67 per cent in US$ realization. Our main market for frozen cuttlefish was European Union with 73.50 per cent, China with 14.45 per cent etc. Exports were made to a total 40 countries during the year 2005-06.

Frozen squid export also recorded an increase of 8.79 per cent, 20.59 per cent, 22.59 per cent and 12.50 per cent in term of quantity, value, US$ and unit value realization respectively. European Union continued to be the main market for Indian frozen squid export with 60.15 per cent followed by USA with 16.45 per cent, Japan with 5.21 per cent etc.

Export of dried items recorded an increase of 46.18 per cent in volume 9.54 per cent in value and 10.86 per cent in US$ realization. Dried items were exported to 36 countries and major players are Honk Kong (33.98 per cent), China (17.65 per cent), Sri Lanka (14.35 per cent), Singapore (8.56 per cent).

Live items exported to 27 countries. It recorded a marginal increase of 13.53 per cent, 21.61 per cent, 23.71 per cent

Table 2.13. Item-wise Export of Marine Products of India during the year 2005-06

Items	% Share to Total		April-March 2005-06	April-March 2004-05	Variation	(%)
1	2		3	4	5	6
Frozen Shrimp	28	Q	145180	138085	7095	5.14
	58.96	V	4272	4220.67	50.84	1.20
	59.02	$	970	938.41	32.01	3.41
		UV$*	7	6.80	0	–1.64
Frozen, Fin Fish	36	Q	182344	159689	22654	14.19
	13.78	V	999	759.27	239.44	31.54
	13.74	$	226	168.70	57.24	33.93
		UV$	1	1.06	0	17.29
Frozen, Cuttle, Fish	10	Q	49651	44239	5412	12.23
	7.58	V	549	474.01	75.13	15.85
	7.57	$	124	104.89	19.59	18.67
		UV$	3	2.37	0	5.74
Frozen, Squid,	10	Q	48124	4228	8.79	
	7.94	V	576	477.26	98.26	20.59
	7.94	$	130	106.63	23.86	22.38
		US$	2	2	0	12.50

Dried items	1	Q	14167	9692	4476	46.18
	0.83	V	133	121.01	11.55	9.54
	0.83	$	30	27.09	2.94	10.86
		UV$	2	3	–1	–24.16
Live items	1	Q	2568	2262	306	13.53
	0.85	V	62	50.75	10.96	21.61
	0.85	$	14	11.31	2.68	23.71
		UV$	5	5.00	0	8.97
Chilled items	1	Q	5060	3988	1072	26.88
	1.13	V	82	68.14	13.42	19.70
	1.12	$	18	15.16	3.25	21.41
		UV$	4	4	0	–4.32
Others	12	Q	60841	55250	5592	10.12
	7.93	V	575	475.58	99.00	20.82
	7.93	$	130	106.29	24.16	22.73
		UV$	2	2	0	11.45
Total	100	Q	512164	461329	50835	11.02
	100	V	7245.30	6646.69	598.61	9.01
	100	$	1644.21	1478.48	165.74	11.21
		UV$	3.21	3.20	0.01	****

Souce: Marine Product Export Development Agency, Cochin, 2006.

(*) UV$ variation % is worked out on the basis of actual value and not on the rounded value.

in quantity, value and US$ realization respectively. Singapore was the main market for Indian live fish (52.68%) followed by Honk Kong (26.52%), Thailand (14.37%) etc.

The export of Chilled fish also increased marginal by 26.88 per cent in volume, 19.70 per cent in value and 21.41 per cent in US$ realization. Chilled fish were exported to 30 countries during the year 2005-06. Major market for chilled fish were Singapore (23.26%). UAE (22.72 per cent), Thailand (15.22%) etc. Other items exported mainly to Japan (41.56%), South East Asia (17.73%), USA (16.17%) etc. which is showrn in Table 2.13.

Major Markets

European Union continued to be the largest market for Indian marine products during the year 2005-06 also. Its share was 26.72 per cent in quantity, 29.46 per cent in value, and 29.44 per cent in US$ realization. It has registered an export growth of 16.22 per cent, 17.31 per cent and 19.39 per cent in quantity, value and US$ realization.

The USA, the second largest market in terms of value had a share of 10.90 per cent, 22.63 per cent and 22.98 per cent in quantity, value and UV$ respectively. It recorded a growth of 11.53 per cent in quantity, 5.34 per cent in value and 7.84 per cent in UV$ terms.

The share of Japan to our export market was 11.67 per cent in quantity, 15.96 per cent in value, and 15.98 per cent in UV$. Export to Japan had shown a negative growth during the year 2005-06 by 3.87 per cent in value and 1.56 per cent in UV$ realization. However, exports in terms of quantity was increased by 3.38 per cent. Export to Middle East countries showed a tremendous growth by 33.96 per cent in quantity, 25.87 per cent in value and 27.30 per cent in UV$ terms. Export to China showed a marginal increase of 9.81 per cent, 22.53 per cent and 27.30 per cent in quantity, value and US$.

Export to Canada, Tunisa, Puertorico, Russia, Lithuania, Reunion, Fuji Island, Bangladesh etc. showed a positive growth, whereas export to Mexico, Cyprus, Australia, Maldives Islands etc. showed a negative trend. Table 2.14 shows the countrywise export of marine products during the year 2005-06.

Performance of Seaports/Airports

Export of marine products has taken place through 18 seaports/airports during the year 2005-06. Two new ports were emerged this period. They are Ahamedabad and Agartala. Chenni kept its position as the largest port in terms of value with a share of 19.17 per cent. However, there was a decline in the export to the tune of 3.51 per cent in value and 1.06 per cent in US$. The largest port in terms of volume was JNP with a share of 23.53 per cent and in value wise it hold third place with a share of 1619 per cent. Kochi continued to be the 2nd largest port in terms of value and third largest port in terms of quantity. Exports from ports Kochi, JNP, Vizag, Pipavav, Mundra, Mangalore/ ICD, Goa, Trivandrum, Calicut etc. registered a positive growth whereas Chennai, Tuticorin, Mumbai, Kandala, Haldia, NSICT, Porbandar etc. showed negative growth. Table 2.15 shows the portwise export of marine products during the year 2005-06.

Socio Economic Profile of Orissa

The State of Orissa popularly known as 'Odisha' is situated on the Eastern coast of Indian peninsula. It is one of the most ancient regions of India with rich tradition and culture. The State comprises of three revenue divisions, 30 districts, 58 sub-divisions, 171 Tahasils, 314 Blocks, 6234 Gram Panchayats and 51,349 villages. Nearly 85 per cent of the population live in the rural area and mostly depend on agriculture and allied activities for their livelihood. The total cultivated land of the State is nearly 58.40 lakh hectares, out of winch only 26.96 lakh hectares were covered under irrigation.

Table 2.14. Country-wise Export of Marine Products of India during the Year 2005-06

Items	% Share to Total		April-March 2005-06	April-March 2004-05	Variation	(%)
1	2		3	4	5	6
Japan	12.00	Q	59785	57832	1953	3.38
	15.96	V	1156	1202.45	–46.49	–3.87
	15.98	$	263	266.96	–4.16	–1.56
USA	11.00	Q	55817	50045	5772	11.53
	22.63	V	1639	1556.09	83.15	5.34
	22.66	$	373	345.52	27.11	7.84
European Union	27.00	Q	136842	117742	19100	16.22
	29.46	V	2134	1819.28	314.97	17.31
	29.44	$	484	405.40	78.63	19.39
China	27.00	Q	137076	124826	12250	9.81
	11.72	V	849	693.25	156.20	22.53
	11.68	$	192	154.10	37.89	24.59
South East Asia	12.00	Q	60140	63842	–3701	–5.08
	8.09	V	586	628.83	–42.98	–6.83
	8.07	$	133	139.77	–7.07	–5.06

1	2		3	4	5	6
Middle East	4.00	Q	22270	16624	5646	33.96
	4.25	V	308	244.42	63.23	25.81
	4.25	$	70	54.70	14.94	27.30
Others	8.00	Q	4.234	30418	9816	32.27
	7.91	V	573	502.37	70.53	14.04
	7.93	$	130	112.03	18.41	16.43
Total	100.00	Q	512164	461329	50835	11.02
	100.00	V	7245.30	6646.69	598.61	9.01
	100.00	$	1644.21	1478.48	165.74	11.1

Souce: Marine product Export Development Agency, Coachin, 2006.

Table 2.15. Portwise export of marine products of India during the year 2005-06.

Items	% Share to Total		April-March 2005-06	April-March 2004-05	Variation	(%)
1	2		3	4	5	6
Chennai	8.83	Q	45246	42649	2597	6.09
	19	V	1382.56	1432.87	–50.31	–3.51
	19	$	315.13	318.55	–3.43	–1.08
Kochi	18.69	Q	957.37	862.91	9446	10.95
	17	V	1218.97	1135.70	83.27	7.33
	17	$	277.06	252.44	24.62	9.75
JNP	23.53	Q	120492	109430	11062	10.11
	16	V	1173.04	965.32	207.73	21.52
	16	$	265.59	215.24	50.35	23.39
Vizag	7.25	Q	37121	32028	5093	15.9
	15	V	1115.30	1029.06	86.23	8.38
	15	$	253.07	228.58	24.50	10.72
Turicorin	5.31	Q	27172	28160	–988	–3.51
	8	V	613.17	635.19	–22.02	–3.47
	8	$	139.27	141.01	–1.74	–1.24

Kolkata	3.57	Q	182.91	18492	–201	–1.09
	7	V	537.95	521.13	16.82	3.23
	7	$	122.18	115.66	6.52	5.64
Pipavav	22.47	Q	115101	109597	5504	5.02
	11	V	776.83	629.54	147.29	23.4
	11	$	174.87	140.83	34.03	24.16
Mundra	3.57	Q	18304	2708	15596	576.02
	2	V	128.67	16.16	112.51	696.23
	2	$	29.27	3.56	25.71	722.61
Mangalore/CD	3.12	Q	15965	10349	5616	54.27
	1	V	103.27	76.92	26.34	34.25
	1	$	23.49	17.15	6.34	36.96
Mumbai	0.63	Q	3224	2744	480	17.5
	1	V	69.17	72.39	–322.07	–4.45
	1	$	15.62	16.17	–0.55	–3.38
Goa	2.09	Q	10719	10030	689	6.87
	1	V	55.56	46.96	8.60	18.31
	1	$	12.59	10.42	2.17	20.83

Count....

Table 2.5 (Count...)

1	2		3	4	5	6
Trivandrum	0.29	Q	1501	1040	461	44.32
	1	V	37.58	21.70	15.87	73.14
	1	$	8.47	4.84	3.63	75.15
Kandla	0.59	Q	3045	6281	–3236	–51.52
	0	V	28.32	51.44	–23.11	–44.94
	0	$	6.49	11.29	–4.79	–42.46
Haldia	0.01	Q	66	113	–47	–41.45
	0	V	1.73	4.18	–2.44	–58.50
	0	$	0.40	0.91	–0.51	–56.03
Calicut	0.01	Q	73	47	27	56.76
	0	V	1.10	0.67	0.44	65.33
	0	$	0.25	0.15	0.10	65.74
Ahamedbad	0.01	Q	35	0	35	****
	0	V	1.06	0	1.06	****
	0	$	0.24	0	0.24	****
Paradeep	0.01	Q	60	0	60	
	0	V	0.98	0.00	0.98	
	0	$	0.23	0.00	0.23	

Agaratala	0.00	Q	11	0	11	****
	0	V	0.04	0.00	0.04	****
	0	$	0.01	0.00	0.01	****
NSICT	0.00	Q	0	6	–6	–100
	0	V	0.00	0.02	–2.02	–100
	0	$	0.00	0.00	0	****
Porbandar	0.00	Q	0	1365	–1365	–100
	0	V	0.00	7.45	–7.45	–100
	0	$	0.00	1.68	–1.68	–100
Total	100	Q	512164	461329	50835	11.02
	100	V	7245.30	6646.69	598.61	9.01
	100	$	1644.21	1478.48	165.74	11.21

Source : Marine product Export Development Agency, Coachin, 2006.

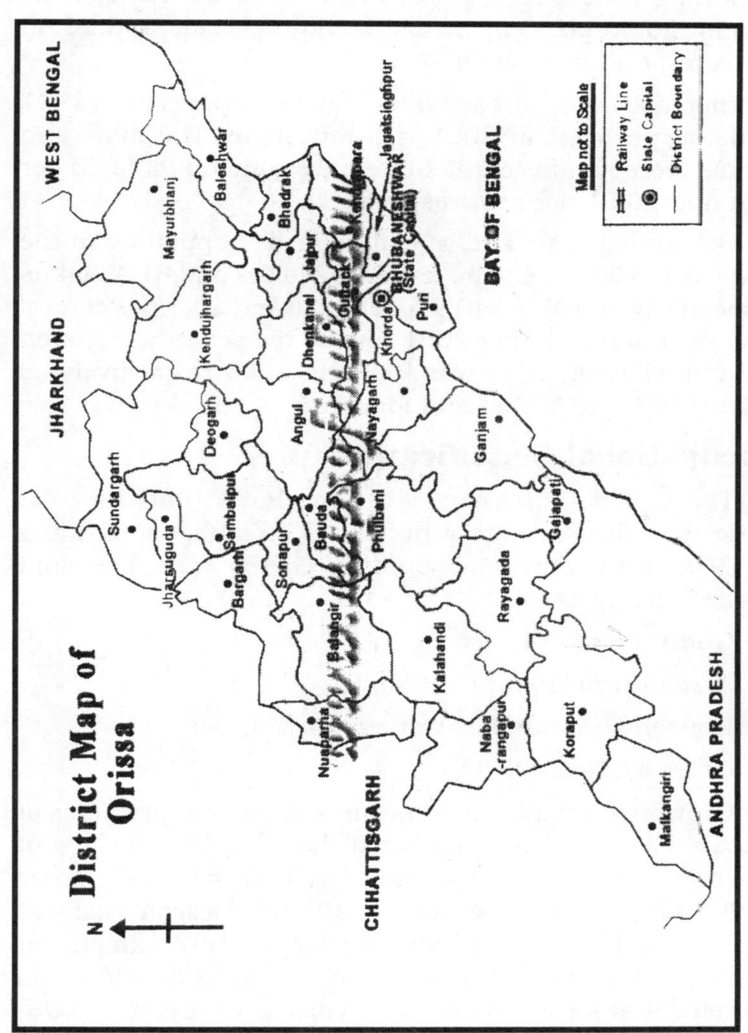

Fig. 2.1 : District Map of Orissa

Demographic Profile

The population of the State is 368.05 lakhs in 2001 exhibiting a decennial growth rate of 16-25 per cent as against 20.06 per cent in the previous decade and 23.86 per cent at all India level.

Increase in the literacy rate from 49.10 per cent in 1991 to 63.08 per cent in 2001 is a milestone. The male and female literacy rates of the State have gone up to 73.35 per cent and 50.51 per cent respectively.

Scheduled caste and scheduled tribe population in the State as per 2001 census, was 60.82 lakhs and 81.45 lakhs respectively, which was 16.5 per cent and 22.1 per cent of total population. As per 2001 census the sex ratio between SC and ST population was 979 and 1003 respectively as against 936 and 978 at all India level.

Occupational Classification

The occupational classification shows that the total workers in the State account for 142.76 lakh, constituting 38.79 per cent of the total population of the State. The main workers comprises of :

Cultivators (35.8%),

Agricultural labour (21.9%),

Household Industries workers (4.2%),

Other workers (38.1%).

Growing unemployment is one of the major problems of the State. It has been estimated that the total backlog of unemployment at the beginning of 2005-06 was of the order 9.90 lakh person years with 1.89 lakh person years of additional labour force during the year and 1.97 lakh person years of employment generation during 2005-06. It is expected that the level of unemployment by the end of 2005-06 will be of the order of 9.82 lakh person per year. To cope with this problem by different self-employment programmes are being complemented by the Government.

The Gross State Domestic Product (GSDP) at constant prices (1993-94) of Orissa has increased from Rs. 18,536.66

crores in 1993-94 to Rs. 29,487.94 crores in 2004-05 registering an annual growth rate of 4.31 per cent over the period. The per capita income has been estimated at Rs. 6,555 in 2004-05. It is very interesting to note that, the food grain production decreased from 71.52 lakh mt in 2003-04 to 69.65 lakh mt during 2004-05.

Agriculture

Agriculture and allied sectors continue to be the main stay of the State's economy with a contribution of about 25.75 per cent to NSDP during 2004-05 at 1993-94 prices. To increase the production the Government has formulated State Agriculture Policy, 1996 with the main objective of doubling the production. This is covered by rice during 2004-05 is 76.9 per cent, followed by pulses 911.2 per cent and oilseeds 5.6 per cent. The area under fibre cultivation accounted for only 1.4 per cent and other crops. Sugarcane, potato, chilli etc. occupy 2.0 per cent of the total cultivated area during 2004-05.

The per capita availability of land in Orissa has considerably gone down from 0.39 hectare in the year 1950-51 to 0.15 hectare in 2004-05 due to increase in population.

Irrigation

In the state, agriculture depends on monsoon. Due to erratic monsoon agricultural production differs from year to year. The net irrigation potential created in the State by the end of 2004-05 from all sources was 26.96 lakh hectares, which is around 46 per cent of the estimated irrigation area of the State. It has been targeted to create 4.65 lakh hectares irrigation potential through major and medium irrigation during the Tenth Plan period.

Animal Resources

Animal resources play an important role in providing income to rural people. As per livestock census conducted the total livestock-population in the State was 240.22 lakh, of which cattle population is counted for 42.8 lakh, buffaloes 14.39 lakh, goats 59.74 lakh, sheep 17.59 lakh and pigs

5.69 lakh. The total milk production in the State was 12.83 lakh tonnes in 2004-05 with per capita availability of 92 g milk per day.

The Tenth Plan targets for milk and egg production is 55.14 lakh mt and 7,506 million nos. respectively.

Forests

The State 58,136 sq. km of forest area which constitutes 37.3 per cent of the State's geographical area. The State forest indicates that out of the recorded forest area of 58,136 sq. km. only 48.366 km (31.06%) of the State,s geographical area is under forest cover. During 2004-05, plantation/ afforestation programme has been carried over an area of 24,605 hectares. The revenue receipt from forest produce which was Rs. 49.81 crore in 2003-04 has increased to 85 crore during 2004-05. *Kendu* leaf is a major source of forest revenue.

Education

Education is one of the important factors for human resource development. The literacy rate in the State has increased from 15.8 per cent in 1951 to 63 per cent in 2001. Dining 2004-05 there are 45,700 primary schools with 52.15 lakh enrolment and 0.99 lakh teacher. The number of upper primary school was 15.893 with 13,83 lakh enrolment and 0.31 lakh teachers. There are 7,141 high schools with 13.25 lakh enrolment and 0.61 lakh teachers in the State. There was one primary school for every 3.7 sq. km, and teacher pupil proportion of 1:41 in 2000-01, it was 3.4 per sq. km and 1:53 respectively during 2004-05. The State has nine universities and 11,680 general colleges. The State has improved in higher education and technical education. The State has three medical colleges, one dental college, one pharmacy college, three ayurvedic colleges, four homoeopathic colleges and one nursing college.

Power

During the year 2004-05 State's share in installed capacity in the State sector was 2798.98 MW against which power was available to the extent of about 1429 MW. Out of 46,989 inhabited villages in the State. 37,744 villages have been electrified by the end of 2004-05, which covers about 81 per cent of the total inhabited villages. An independent regulatory authority has been established to administer, regulate and monitor generation, transmission and distribution of power.

Transport and Communication

Orissa is a backward state. In this regard as per the estimates of Planning Commission about 40 per cent of the villages in Orissa have all weather road as compared to 60 per cent in all India level. The road length in the State was 2.37 lakh km in 2004-05. At the end of 2004-05 total railway route lengths in Orissa was 2287 km including 91 km of narrow gauge railway. During 2004-05 about 14.61 lakh motor vehicles were on road in the State. The number of motor vehicles per thousand sq. km was 9383 and per lakh population was 3894.

Out of 11 major ports in the country Paradeep is the only major port belonging to Orissa. During 2004-05, the export and import of goods were 216.66 lakh and 84.38 lakhs respectively through this port in the State as against 186.08 lakh mt of good exported and 67.03 lakh mt goods imported during 2003-04.

Health Service

The National Health Policy aims at providing health care and medical service to all sections of the society. By the end of 2004-05, there were 174 hospitals, 231 community health centres, 120 Primary Health Centres (PHCs). In the State, 1182 PHCs (New) and 14 mobile health units providing curative health service. The family welfare programme was implemented by the State. The death rate per thousand has been brought down from 10.05 to 9.7 during the period 2002-03 and the infant mortality rate has been reduced from 97 per thousand live births in 1999 to 83 thousand live births in 2003.

Minerals

The State has vast mineral resources such as coal, iron ores, manganese, bauxite, chromite etc. According to all India mineral resources estimate the mineral deposit of Orissa in respect of chromite, nickel, bauxite, iron ore are about 97.37 per cent, 95.10 per cent, 49.74 per cent and 33.91 per cent respectively of the total deposits of India. During 2004-05 the mineral production of the State was 1270.48 lakh ton valued at Rs. 6148.61 crores. The export of minerals and ores to different countries during 2004-05 was 171.67 lakh ton. Mining royalties and other revenue collected during 2004-05 stood at Rs. 670.51 crores as against Rs. 550.76 crores in 2003-04 showing an increase of 21.74 per cent.

Industry

With vast mineral resources and other infrastructural facilities and manpower the State has an immense potential for industrialization. Large industries such as Rourkela Steel plant, NALCO, IRE, Paradeep Phosphates, Coal-based power plant at Talcher, Kanhia, and Banharpal has been set up in the State during different Plan periods. By the end of 2004-05, Orissa has 362 large and medium industries with an investment of Rs. 3,600.21 crores and employment potential for 85,926 persons. During this period 4511 small industries with an investment of Rs. 245.59 crores were set up in the state producing employment to 21,898 persons. Besides 17,808 cottage industries have been setup in the State with an investment of Rs 47.11 crore and creating employment for 29,587 persons during 2004-05. During 2004-05 120.86 lakh sq. m of cloth was produced providing employment to 1.03 lakh persons by the handloom industiy in the state.

Poverty Alleviation

The most important problem of the State is poverty. Orissa is the poorest among major States with 47.15 per cent people living below the poverty line. Several Central-sponsored programmes such as SGSY and SGRY has been functioning in the State. During 2004-05 about 553.954 lakh man days of employment have been generated under, SGRY. The State Government is also poised to implement the Employment Guarantee Act from 2006-07. State Government have constituted a Poverty Task Force (PTF) headed by Development Commissioner to devise an actionable poverty reduction strategy, PTF is taking steps to reduce poverty by at least 7 per cent at a simple rate of 1.4 per cent per year during the Tenth Plan period.

Welfare of Scheduled Castes and Scheduled Tribes

As per the 2001 census S.C. population was 16.5 per cent and ST's population was 22.1 per cent. Various special programmes and welfare measures have been launched for their benefit. It includes legal aid, rehabilitation of victimised STs and SCs, housing facilities, establishment of special employ-ment, reservation in employment etc.

Externally Aided Projects

In order to bridge the gap for development project, the State avails financial assistance from various external sources like Germany, World Bank, DFID, JICA, JBIC etc. Eighteen Internally Aided Project (EAP) which include seven ongoing projects and eleven pipeline projects are programmed for implementation during the Annual Plan 2005-06 covering sectors like works, irrigation, H&UD, Forestry, Rural Development, welfare of SCs & STs etc.

Fisheries

The fisheries boundries of the state Orissa can be broadly divided into two parts namely (*a*) South Orissa and (*b*) North Orissa.

South Orissa: It includes Ganjam, Puri and the Southern parts of Cuttack district. It has a narrow continental shelf with open sandy beaches. The entire coastal belt of Cuttack district is lying with two districts *i.e.,* Kendrapara and Jagatsinghpur.

North Orissa: North Orissa consists of Northern Cuttack

district and Balasore which are characterized by an extended continental shelf, tidal areas and extensive river deltas. From 1993-94 onwards Balasore district has been bifurcated into new districts, Balasore and Bhadrak. It is shown in Table 2.16.

Table 2.16. Name of the Species in Ganjam, Puri, Cuttack *and* Balasore of Orissa

Name of the District	Species
Balasore	Hilsa, Catfish, Prawn and sciaenids
Ganjam	Elasmobranchs, pomfret
Puri	Scianeids
Cuttack	Scianeids, prawn, catfish, pomfrets

Source: District Fisheries Office.

Table 2.16 reflects the districts with spices. It shows that Hilsa, Catfish, Prawns are available in Balasore, pomfret, Elasmobranchs are available in Ganjam, Scianeids are available in Puri while Scianeids, Prawn, Catfish, pomfrets are available in Cuttack district.

Fisheries in Orissa : A Profile

After the formation of a separate State of Orissa in 1936, the fisheries section was started under the Directorate of Industries. However, the Department of Fisheries, Forestry and Agriculture was established in the year 1960. Then fishing was separated from this department and finally re-christened as Department of Fisheries and Animal Resources in the year 1990-91 for the development of fishery resources.

The basic objectives of the Department of Fisheries for the development of fisheries sector in the State are:

1. Gainful utilization of the physical resources.
2. Increase fish production by introducing new production and harvesting techniques.

3. Introduction of efficient, skill and technical know-how about modern system of distribution and marketing to promote per capita consumption of fish.
4. Improvement for the socio-economic development of fishing communities and lastly.
5. Promotion of export to earn foreign exchange for the country.

Fishery, an allied sector of agriculture in Orissa is gradually drawing attention as an important area for employment and income generation. Orissa being abundant with water resources has enough scope and potentiality in fishing. With the introduction of improved technology public interest in fishing activities is rising.

Table 2.17. Fishermen Statistics of Orissa

(in No)

Total fishermen population	10,15,170
Total marine population	3,32,772
Total male fishermen	53,020
Total female fishermen	94,491
Total children	86,140
Total Active population	1,52,141
Total Ancillary population	86,312
Women population	33,309
Total no. of Inland population	14,405
Total no. of households	6,82,398
Total male fishermen	2,27,286
Total female fishermen	1,96,856
Total children	2,58,256
Total active population	1,89,420
Total women population	92,750

Source : Hand book on Fisheries Statistics, Orissa, 2001-01, P-66.

Orissa having a coastline of 480 km and abundant inland water coverage has excellent scope and potentialities for development of the fishery sector. The State has 6,70,017 hectare of fresh water area and 4,17,537 hectare of brackish water area. Orissa occupies 7th position with the fishermen population mentioned in Table 2.17.

Table 2.17 gives fishermen's statistics in Orissa. It includes inland and marine sectors. The State has a total of 3878 fishermen villages out of which number 589 maxine village and 3289 inland villages.

The total fishermen's population is about 3 per cent of the State's total population with 2.04 per cent consisting of inland fishermen and the rest marine fishermen. In spite of aboundant resources; the economic status of fishermen is below the poverty line (BPL). Therefore, all out efforts are being made by the State Government to boost up the fisheries sector with the introduction of improved technology but keeping the ecological balance intact.

Plan Outlay

The following is the plan outlay and expenditure made during different plan period. Which is showrn in Table 2.18.

Table 2.18 shows plan outlay and expenditure of fisheries of the state under different plan period

Fishery Policy

For the increase of fish production and welfare of the fishing community as a whole, the, Government has formulated policy for the fishery, with a view to increase fish production in the State. The Government has formulated policy for the fishery development of Orissa. The policy aims at:

(*i*) increasing fish production by adopting scientific methods of culture.

(*ii*) assisting fishermen in more efficient fishing.

(*iii*) boosting fishing operations in deep sea culture and capture to fishermen and farmers.

(*iv*) Transmitting technology both for capture and culture fishery to fishermen and fish culture.

(*iv*) establishing fish feed mills for culture of fish and prawn.

Table 2.18. Plan Outlay and Expenditure (Rs. In lakh)

SI. No.	Plan period	State Plan outlay (Revise)	Expenditure
1.	1st Plan (1951-52 to 56-56)	33.69	28.72
	2nd Plan (1956-57 to 60-61)	77.25	79.36
	3rd Plan (1961-62 to 65-66)	186.00	200.20
4.	1966-67 (Annual Plan)	55.19	33.55
5.	1967-68 (Annual Plan)	43.12	41.47
6.	1968-69 (Annual Plan)	25.65	19.63
7.	4th Plan (1967-68 to 73-74)	225.00	172.61
8.	5lh Plan (1974-75 to 77-78)	270.00	173.26
9.	1978-79 (Annual plan)	140.00	134.98
10.	1979-80 (Annual plan)	143.00	136.70
11.	6th Plan (1980-81 to 84-85)	1015.00	963.68
12.	7th Plan (1985-86 to 89-90)	2693.08	2671.39
13.	1990-91 (Annual plan)	940.00	886.21
14.	1991-92 (Annual plan)	888.00	835.65
15.	8th Plan (1992-93 to 96-97)	7705.03	5102.80
16.	9th Plan (1997-98 to 01-02)	11966.79	7002.27
17.	1997-98 (Annual Plan)	1939.12	828.54
18.	1998-99 (Annual Plan)	1934.64	1411.92
19.	1999-2000 (Annual Plan)	1824.14	964.94
20.	2000-2001 (Annual Plan)	2361.83	1753.27
21.	2001-2002 (Annual Plan)	622.03	681.82

Source : Hand Book on Fisheries Statistics Orissa, 2000-01, p-1.

Efforts are being made to step up fish seeds production as well as fish production to create self-employment opportunities and to increase per capita income by utilizing unexploited water resources through application of new technologies and expansion of infrastrural facilities during Tenth Five-year Plan period. It is proposed to give priority to the following activities:

1. Increase in production of fish seed in private sector by 1.25 crores.
2. Increase of water area by 2,500 he under aquaculture sector.
3. Culture-based capture fishery in 11 reservoirs of KBK districts under RLTAP programme.
4. Development of reservoir fisheries in non-KBK district through a suitable reservoir fishery policy.
5. Development of freshwater prawn culture.
6. To provide trading and employment opportunities.
7. To provide incentives for production offish seed and fish on commercial basis.
8. Enforcement of Orissa Marine Regulation Act/Rules with due care for endangered species like Olive Ridley Turtles for sustainable fisheries to improve living condition of marine fishermen with special emphasis on health, hygiene and sanitation.
9. Strengthening of infrastructure in inland fish marketing.
10. Provision of infrastructure facilities for pisci-culture.

Fish Production in Orissa

The fish production in Orissa is showrn in Table 2.19.

Table 2.19 shows that out of 30 districts the above table indicates Balasore hold the first position and Rayagada holds the last position in production of fish. It includes both, marine water and brackish water. Total fish production of Orissa is depicted in Table 2.20.

Table 2.19. Fish Production in Orissa.

(In '000 mt tonnes)

Sl. No.	Year	Fresh Water	Marine Water	Brackish Water	Total
1	2	3	4	5	6
	1996-97	127293.40	133462.00	1602.46	276957.86
	1997-98	135636.00	156080.00	16783.00	308398.00
	1998-99	145006.00	124329.00	14898.00	284233.00
	1999-02	124861.00	125935.00	10442.00	261238.00
	2000-01	125114.48	121088.00	13347.96	259550.44
	2001-02	147400.00	113893.00	20660.00	281953.00
	2002-03	154237.00	11500.89	19963.00	289210.27
	2003-04	16559.99	116880.39	24477.38	306949.76
	2004-05	—	—	—	—
	Districts				
01.	Angul	5781.08	0.00	0.00	5781.08
02.	Balasore	7542.97	30061.01	2042.87	39646.08
03.	Baraghar	8251.57	0.00	0.00	8253.57
04.	Bhadrak	6446.14	10001.00	1598.86	18046.57
05.	Bolangir	8432.46	0.00	0.00	8432.46
06.	Boudh	2778.35	0.00	0.00	2778.35
07.	Cuttack	69621.06	0.00	0.00	6921.06
08.	Deogarh	3287.94	0.00	0.00	3287.94
09.	Dhenkanal	6579.45	0.00	0.00	6579.45
10.	Gajapati	1187.93	0.00	0.00	1187.93
11.	Ganjam	1717.07	9175.63	1648.77	27998.47
12.	Jagatsinghpur	5931.70	29344.17	2330.20	37606.07
13.	Jajpur	4148.68	0.00	0.00	4148.68
14.	Jharsuguda	2824.03	0.00	0.00	2824.03
15.	Kalahandi	8362.91	0.00	0.00	8362.91
16.	Kandhamal	939.84	0.00	0.00	939.84
17.	Kendrapara	5981.03	10759.03	1686.50	18505.53

1	2	3	4	5	6
18.	Keonjhar	5622.07	0.00	0.00	5622.07
19.	Khunda	6170.97	0.00	0.00	193310.91
20.	Koraput	2400.15	0.00	0.00	2400.15
21.	Malkangiri	3979.83	0.00	0.00	3979.83
22.	Mayurbhanj	9909.04	0.00	0.00	9909.04
23.	Nabarangpur	3200.88	0.00	0.00	3200.88
24.	Nayagarh	6302.25	0.00	0.00	6302.25
25.	Nuapada	2209.04	0.00	0.00	2209.15
26.	Puri	6533.32	27503.55	2009.24	36046.11
27.	Rayagada	609.22	0.00	0.00	609.22
28.	Sambalpur	7300.47	0.00	0.00	730047
29.	Sonepur	4793.61	0.00	0.00	4793.61
30.	Sundargarh	4487.42	0.00	0.00	4487.47

Source: Statistical Abstract of Orissa, 2005, p. 75.

Table 2.20 shows that as per Fisheries Department Total fish production in the State is in increasing trend. Fish production suffered in 1999-2000 and 2000-01 due to super cyclone, but thereafter it is showing an increasing trend. It is mounted to 315.80 thousand mt in 2004-05, registering an increase of about 2.88 per cent over 2003-04. The total value of fish produced in the State has increased by 2.46 per cent from Rs. 1230.23 crore during 2003-04 to Rs. 1260.46 crores during 2004-05, while the value of inland fish production decreased by 0.20 per cent over 2003-04. The brackish water fish production has decreased in 2004-05 to 23.78 mt tonnes but the value of marine fish production has increased by 9.82 per cent during the same period. As per Fisheries Department total fish production in the State is increasing.

The percapita annual consumption of fish in the State has increased from 8.28 kg in 2003-04 to 8.35 kg in 2004-05. Table 2.21 presents the year-wise disposition offish.

Table 2.20. Total Fish Production of Orissa ('000 mt. tonnes)

Sl. No.	Year	Inland fish production			Marine fish	Total (5 + 6)	Crab production
		Fresh Water	Brackish Water	Total			
1	2	3	4	5	6	7	8
1.	1999-2000	124.86	10.44	135.30	125.94	261.24	0.54
2.	2000-2001	124.11	13.44	138.55	121.09	259.64	1351.35
3.	2001-2002	147.40	20.66	168.061	13.89	281.95	1.15
4.	2002-2003	154.42	19.96	174.38	115.01	289.39	2.23
5.	2003-2004	165.59	24.48	190.07	116.88	306.95	2.20
6.	2004-2005	170.09 (2.72)	23.78 (–2.80)	193.87 (2.00)	121.93 (4.32)	315.80 (2.88)	1.72

Figures in parentheses indicate percentage of change over previous year.
Source: Economic Survey, 2005-06, Government of Orissa, p. 712.

Out of the total 315.80 tmt fish produced in the State during 2004-05, about 270.27 tmt (85.6%) was marked in raw form, 17.27 tmt in freezing, 13.64 tmt (4.3%) for salt drying corking. The quantity marketed in raw form during 2004-05 has increased 2.89 per cent over 2003-04.

Disposition of Fish Produced in Orissa

The fish produced in Orissa is disposed in different ways which is shown in Table 2.21.

Table 2.21. Disposition of Fish Produced in Orissa

(in thousand MT)

Sl. No.	Year	Marketed in Raw fish	Free-zing	Drying	Salt-ing	Can-ning	Total
1.	1999-00	208.40	14.60	32.90	5.30	—	261.20
2.	2000-01	206.70	15.70	27.80	930	0.10	259.60
3.	2001-02	229.02	16.03	26.80	10.07	0.03	281.95
4.	2002-03	246.39	16.56	17.60	8.66	—	289.21
5.	2003-04	262.68	16.76	13.27	14.21	—	306.95
6.	2004-05	270.27	17.27	13.64	14.62	—	315.80

Source: Economic Survey 2005-06. Government of Orissa, p. 7/4.

Table 2.21 shows the disposition of fish produced in Orissa. Last three years, it has shows an increasing trend, which is a good sign for Orissa's fisheries. It increases from 261.20 thousand mt in 1999-2000 to 315.80 tmt in 2004-05.

Inland Fisheries

The inland fisheries can be classified broadly into two categories: (*i*) fresh water fisheries and (*ii*) brackish water fisheries. The fresh water fishing sources comprises as per the information given in Table 2.22 and Table 2.23.

Table 2.2 shows that the total fishing covers 670,017 hectares. It includes tanks, ponds, reservoirs, lakes, swamps, jheels, rivers & canals.

Table 2.22. Total Fishing Area of Orissa

(In Hectrares)

(*i*)	Small and big tanks and ponds	1,18,452
(*ii*)	Medium and large reservoirs (areas above 10 ha)	2,00,379
(*iii*)	Lakes, swamps, J heels	1,80,000
(*iv*)	River and Canals	1,71,186
	Total	670,017

Source: Official records of Directorate of Fisheries of Orissa

Table 2.23. Brackish Water Statistics of Orissa Area

(in Hectares)

(*i*)	Chilika Lake	79,000
(*ii*)	Easturies	2,97,850
(*iii*)	Brackish water tanks	32,587
(*iv*)	Back water	8,100
	Total	4,17,537

Source: Handbook on Fisheries Statistics, Orissa, 2000-01, pp. vi-vii.

Table 2.23 shows that the total brackish water comprises of 4,17.537 hectares of water. Chilika lake plays an important role in this regard. For development of inland fisheries in the State, it has been proposed to continue different ongoing schemes such as production of quality prawn, development of reservoir fisheries through FFDA etc. during 2004-2005.

Fresh Water Fisheries

The fresh water fish production in the State at the end of Ninth Plan period was 147.4 tmt, increased of 15.8 per cent to, production achieved at the end of Eighth Plan period. Fresh water fish production was highest in Ganjam District (17.81 tmt) and lowest in Rayagad district (0.89 tmt) during 2004-05. Table 2.24 below shows the fish production from different sources in Orissa since 1999-2000.

Table 2.24. Fresh water Fish Production From Different Source in Orissa

(in '000 mt)

Sl. No.	Year	Tanks/ ponds	Reser-voir	Lakes/ swamps	River/ Canal	Total
1.	1999-2000	88.11	13.81	2.07	20. 87	124.86
2.	2000-2001	92.44	8.01	2.73	21.93	125.11
3.	2001-2002	112.85	7.09	4.00	23.46	147.40
4.	2002-2003	119.80	8.50	2.67	23.27	154.24
5.	2003-2004	133.62	10.14	2.76	19.08	165.59
6.	2004-2005	140.46	11.53	1.79	16.31	170.09

Source: Economic Survey 2005-06, Government of Orissa, Bhubaneswar P-7/4.

Table 2.24 shows an increase of fish production in the State from 1999-2000 which is a good sign for the economic development of the State.

A Centrally-sponsored scheme, "Fish Farmers Development Agencies Scheme (FFDAS)" is being implemented in the State to develop pond areas and to impart training to fish farmers in modern pisciculture techniques. A total of 30 FFDAS are functioning in the State. By the end of 2004-05, 54,769 hectares of tank areas and 48,396 fish agencies have been developed to boost up production of fish. During 2004-05, 628.40 hectares of tank area has been developed and 1483 fish farmers have been trained with an expenditure of Rs. 183.31 lakhs under State's share and Rs. 116.05 lakhs from Central share. It has been targeted to develop 12,500 hectares of water area and to train 1500 fish farmers during the Tenth Plan period.

Fresh water prawn culture programme, which has been launched since 1991-92 is widely accepted by the fish farmers of the state. Demand for prawn from both within and outside of the State is high and this activity generates good profit for the farmers. About 108.0 lakh of fresh water prawn seeds were collected and distributed among the fish farmers during the year 2004-05 against the target of 108.50 lakhs.

In order to meet the growing demand for quality fish seed in the State, emphasis has been given for production of quality fish seed in 19 departmental hatcheries, five hatcheries of Orissa Pisciculture Development Corporation and 22 hatcheries in private sector. During 2004-05, about 60.48 crore-quality fish have been produced and sold to pisciculturist for stock in their tanks.

Reservoirs of Orissa

There are different reservoirs in the State which is shown in Table 2.25.

Table 2.25 Reservoirs of Different Districts in Orissa

Sl.No.	District	Reservoir
1.	Nayagarh	Kuanria Budhabudhiani Betabana Baghua Koska
2.	Mayurbhanj	Kalo Badjore Bainkabal Haladia Paunsia Nesa Khadkei Sunei
3.	Ganjam	Bhanjanagar Sorada Doha Ghodahad Dhanei Salia R.N. Sagar
4.	Kandhmal	Pilasalki
5.	Nuapada	Saipala Sundar Patora

Sl.No.	District	Reservoir
6.	Kalahandi	Churiagarh Bhatrajore Karanjkote
7.	Nawarangpur	Bahskel Indravati (K) Indravati
8.	Koraput	Upper Kolab Kodigaon J. Sagar
9.	Malkanagiri	Satiguda
10.	Gajapati	Harabhangi
11.	Anugul	Derjang
12.	Dhenkanal	Dadanaghati Sarapa
13.	Sambalpur	Bankasal
14.	Bargarh	Kumbha Jhanbandha Padmapur nala Khandijharan Talkhol
15.	Sundargarh	Talsara Saratgarh Pitamahal
16.	Keonjhar	Kanjhari Ramial Remal
17.	Jharsuguda	Jambunalla
18.	Deogarh	Cohira
19.	Sonepur	Harihajore

Source: Hand Book on Fisheries Statistics Orissa, 2000-01, p. 36.

Table 2.25 indicates that Mayurbhanj has the highest 8 reservoirs, while Kandhamala, Jharsuguda, Deogonh and sonepur has only one reservoir each.

State Reservoir Fishery Policy, Orissa

The State Reservoir Fishery Policy, Orissa has been formed with a view to introduce scientific pisciculture in reservoir and thereby to create employment opportunities. There are 53 reservoirs in Orissa as per the list of Government. The objectives of this policy are:

1. To increase fish production from the vast untapped and under tapped reservoir resources through scientific management.
2. To generate gainful rural employment with special reference to fishing communities and economic rehabilitation of displaced persons.
3. To produce systematic management strategies both for conservation and sustained fish production.
4. To attract investments from the private sector.
5. To stimulate entrepreneurship for fishery sector with special reference to reservoir fishery.
6. To substitute traditional methods by introduction of advanced technology for reservoir fishery.
7. To generate substantial revenue for the State. This policy permits transfer of reservoir with an area of 100 acres and above to the fisheries and Animal Resources Department, Government of Orissa. The F&A.R.D. Department, Government of Orissa has been empowered to lease out these reservoirs to the primary fishermen Co-operative societies, registered under the Orissa Self-help Co-operative Act. The policy would give preference to displaced persons/project affected persons.

Brackish Water Fisheries

For ensuring development of fisheries programme in the State, a project was launched with the World Bank assistance during 1992-93 at an estimated cost of Rs. 70.13 crores. The project aims at development of brackish water area for shrimp culture and reservoir for exploiting fishing resources. Under this programme, the brackish water shrimp culture unit has already been set up at Jagatpore and Banapada in Kendrapara district at a cost of Rs. 25.27 crore where 405 ponds each with 0.5 hectares area and 76 ponds with one hectares area have been excavated and put into culture through private entrepreneurs or farmers. Table 2.26 shows total brackish area resources of Orissa.

Table 2.26. Brackish Water Resources of Orissa.

Shrimp Culture Area	38575
Government	29637
Private	8938
Area suitable for shrimp culture	32618
Govt.	24031
Private	8587
Area developed for shrimp Culture	53727
Extensive	4362
Modified Extensive	373
Semi intensive	637
Extensive Ghery culture	7338
Area under culture	6038
Extensive	3848
Modified extensive	386
Semi extensive	642
Extensive Ghery culture	1162
Back waters	810

Source: Official records of Directorate of Fisheries, Orissa.

Table 2.26 shows total brackish water area suitable for fishermen of the State. Brackish Water Fisheries Development Agencies (BWFDA) have been setup in seven coastal districts of the State, which work for development of brackish water fish farming with special emphasis of prawn culture. The total brackish water area of the State is around 4.18 lakh hectares including shrimps culture areas. Out of the total number of estuaries brackish water lake and backwaters, the Brackish Water Fisheries Development Agencies have identified 32,587 hectares as suitable for prawn culture.

These agencies have developed about 13,635,17 hectares for prawn culture by the end of 2004-05. Brackish water prawn culture was undertaken in an area of 8.012 hectares and 7,875 mt brackish water prawn was produced. About 10,053 fish farmers were benefited and 4,793 fanners were trained in modern shrimp culture techniques. Loans, amounting to Rs. 11.91 crore, was released by different banks to these beneficiaries and an amount of Rs. 2.46 crore had been given as subsidy up to the end of March 2005 since the inception of the programme. It has been targeted to develop 1000 hectares of brackish water area and to train 1050 fish farmers during the Tenth Plan period. During 2005-06 it has been programmed to develop 200 hectares of brackish water area and to train 300 beneficiaries. Further, a target for production of shrimp culture has been fixed at 8,000 mt during 2005-06.

Table 2.27. Brackish Water Fish/Shrimp/Crab Production from Different Sources

in Orissa (in mt)

Sl. No.	Year	Chilika Lake	Brackish Water shrimp	Estuaries	Total Production
1.	1999-2000	1,745	3,081	5,616	10,442
2.	2000-2001	4,983	6,430	2,029	13,442
3.	2001-2002	11,989	7,204	1,467	20,660
4.	2002-2003	10,894	7,172	1,898	19,964
5.	2003-2004	24,053	8,112	2,312	24,447
6.	2004-2005	13,260	7,875	2,641	23,776

Source: Economic Survey 2005-06, Government of Orissa, Bhubaneswar, p. 7-8.

During 2004-05, about 4,921 lakh brackish water prawn seeds were supplied to the prawn farmers of the State.

There are 12 brackish water prawn hatcheries in the State of which the departmental hatchery at Chandrabhaga has produced 20.58 lakh Shrimp seeds, during 2004-05, which were sold to the fanners. For 2005-06 there is a target for production of 60 lakh shrimp/prawn seeds. This is shown in Table 2.27.

Table 2.27 shows a decrease in production in the year 2001-05. This is due to fall in production in Chilika Lake drastically from 24,053 mt in 2005-06 to 13.260 mt in 2004-05.

Chilika Lake

Geographically the lake is situated at 85″6′ to 85″38′ East longitude and 19″28′ to 19″54′ North latitude. The average water spread area is 906 sq. km during summer and 1165 sq. km during monsoon. The average depth of water in summer is 0.93 metre to 2.63 m and the average depth of water in monsoon is 1.73 m to 3.7 m. The length of the outer channel is 35 km. The number of lake mouths at present is 3 at Sipakuda (New) Palur Channel and near Moto village. Four tributaries i.e Daya, Bhargavi, Luna, Ratnachira from North East sector and other two i.e. Salia and Kansari from Southwest sector are connected to the Lake. The total inland area is 223 sq. km. There are 132 fishermen villages consisting of 22,032 families and 1,22,339 population of which 30,936 fishermen entirely depend on Chilika lake for their livelihood. From the total population 34,654 are male, 31,588 are female and the rest are children belonging to fishermen community The total number of boats used are 56. The number of motorized boats are 24 and traditional boats are 32. The fishermen used different types of gears for their fishing activities.

The total number of nets used is 872. They are gill net, trap net, body net, drag net, Bhaech Jal, Gania Jal, stick net, casrnet etc. The fishermen use different fishing methods like bahani, hook and line, Gill net, khanda jal (trap fishing) by poloha. There are 99 primary cooperative societies comprising of 27,490 members. There are 18 landing centres in which about 13,098 mt offish or shrimps and 162 mt of crab are landed in 2004-05.

Marine Fisheries

The State has a coastline of 480 km. with a continental shelf area of about 24,000 sq km, which comprises about six per cent of the coastline and 4.7 per cent of the continental shelf area of the country. Table 2.28.

Table 2.28. Coastal Length of Different Districts in Orissa.

District	Coast length (in km)
Balasore	80
Bhatirak	50
Kendrapara	68
Jagatsmghpur	67
Puri	155
Ganjam	480

Source: Official records of Director of Fisheries, Orissa.

Table 2.28 shows the coastal length of different districts of Orissa. District Ganjam occupies the first position with a coastal length of 480 km while district Jagatsinghpur held the sixth position.

The continental self area of the State are depicted in Table 2.29.

Table 2.29. The Continental Shelf Area in Different Depth Zones

(in mtr)

	Depth Zones
0-20	6820
20-50	8650
50-100	4810
100-200	3550
Total	23,830

Source: Marine Fishery Resource of Orissa—*West Bengal Coast*, Bulletin, 19th Nov. 1990, Fishery Survey of India, Government of India

Table 2.29 reflects continental shelf area in different depth zones of the State.

About 121.93 tmt of fish was caught from marine sector during 2004-05 out of which prawn, clupeids, scianeids, catfishes and Pomfrets are some of the important species.

The Orissa Marine Fishing Act is being implemented in the State to safeguard the coastal water areas of the State. Registration of Trawlers, renewal of licensses and conservation of the endangered species of fish and turtles are being taken up. Fishing jetties are constructed to provide fish landing facilities at Talasari, Kirtania, Pentahkata, Gopalpur on sea await completion. Fishing Jetty at Nairi has been completed and handed over to Managing Director, Fish Fed for Operation. Two schemes namely small landing central/berthing facilities and fishing harbours, have been merged and a the new scheme is launched as "Establishment of Fishing Harbour and Fish Landing Centre". Outlay and expenditure under the scheme during 2004-05 is given in Table 2.30.

Table 2.30. Outlay/Expenditure During the Year 2004-05

(Rs. in lakh)

Item	Outlay	Sanctioned	Expenditure
State Plan	20.00	14.43	14.43
Centerally sponsered Plan	173.76	—	—
Total	193.76	14.43	14.43

Source: Economic Survey 2005-06, Government of Orissa, p. 7/9.

Table 2.30 above shows outlay of funds and sanction of fund during the year 2004-05. It clearly shows that the total outlay is 193.76 lakh, sanctioned amount is 14.43 lakhs.

In view of the importance of the fisheries sector in the States economy, the plan investment for development of fisheries has been increased from Rs. 0.29 crore during the first plan period. The annual outlay expenditure during 2004-05 is given in Table 2.31.

Table 2.31. Outlay/Expenditure during the year 2004-05

(Rs. in Crores)

Sl. No.	Share	Revised outlay	Amount Sanctioned	Expen-diture
1.	State plan	3.79	3.39	3.39
2.	Centrally-sponsored plan	6.09	1.86	1.86
	Central plan	0.48	0.07	0.07

Source : Economic Survey, Government of Orissa, 2005-06, p. 7/9

Table 2.31 shows the outlay from State Plan and Centrally sponsored Plan and the Central Plan the amount sanctioned for expenditure.

Both freshwater and brackish water prawn culture have assumed considerable importance on account of their profitability as well as their foreign exchange earning capabilities. In the meantime, private entrepreneurs have set up prawn seed hatcheries in Puri and Ganjam districts to cater the needs of prawn farmers. There is a Government shrimp hatchery at Chandrabhaga in Puri district and another at Gopalpur in Ganjam district under the Marine Product Export Development Agency (MPEDA). Besides 12 other private shrimp hatcheries are established at different areas of Gopalpur, Konark and Puri. The Fisheries Department also has a freshwater prawn hatchery at Paradeep.

Development of Pisciculture under Revised Long-term Action Plan for KBK District

Development of pisciculture under RLTAP aims at promoting fisheries sector to raise income of the people of KBK districts. During 2004-05, it is proposed to develop 34 reservoirs with water spread area of 1,558 hectares under culture based capture fisheries in reservoir of KBK districts under RLTAP programme.

Export and Import Of Fish

The marine product from Orissa is being exported to foreign countries such as Japan, China, U.S.A., U.K., U.A.E.,

Indonesia, Hong Kong, etc. over the years. Frozen marine products such as shrimps fish, sea fish, cattle fish, crab etc are exported to these countries. But the export of frozen shrimps constitutes the major portion of the amount of marine produces over the year. In the year 2005-06 the total export of fish was estimated at 86.799 mt.

About 37.01 tmt of freshwater fish was imported through private trade channels from the neighboring states in 2004-05 as against 34.59 tmt of fresh water fish imported during 2003-04. This indicates that the demand for fish from fresh water in the State is more than the production.

Fishermen Welfare Schemes

The Accident Insurance Scheme has been introduced in 1983-84 in the State. Under this scheme a fisherman's life is insured and an amount Rs. 50,000 is provided in the event of his accidental death or permanent disability and up to Rs. 25,000 in the event of partial disability The premium of Rs.14 for insurance coverage for each fisherman is paid by the State Government and the Government of India on 50 : 50 basis. During 2004-05, 1.20 lakh fishermen were covered under the scheme. There are 977 primary fishermen co-operative societies, central PFCS and APEX society registered by the end of 2004-05 in the State with 1,10,651 members, 199 and 334 members respectively. There is further need to organize fish farmers in all the three sectors at marine, brackish and inland fisheries and more group schemes can be launched.

Contribution of Orissa in Fish Production

Orissa plays an important role in fish production from the year 1995-96 to 2004-05. Which is shown in Table-2.32.

Table 2.32 reveals that contribution of Orissa in fish font production is gradually increasing from 39% during the year 1995-96 to 47% during the year 2004-05. The total fish production has also increased from 1,00,036 mt in 1995-96 to 1,47,417 in 2004-05.

Table 2.32. The Contribution of Orissa in Fish Production

(In mt)

Year	Production from fresh water	Production from brackish water	Total Production	% of pisci-culture	% of total production
1995-96	93079	6957	100036	74	39
1996-97	92927	6627	99554	69	36
1997-98	99980	4873	104853	69	34
1998-99	98386	6256	104642	65	37
1999-02	88105	3081	91186	67	35
2000-01	92439	6430	98869	71	38
2001-02	112845	7204	120049	71	43
2002-03	119795	7172	126967	73	44
2003-04	133617	8112	141729	75	46
2004-05	140250	7166	147416	76	47

Source: Compiled from official recors of directorate of Fisheries, Orissa.

Chapter 3

Socio-economic Condition of Fishermen of Sample District

Introduction

Geographical profile of the district is considered as the most important study of the socio-economic conditions of the agrarian labouress of Ganjam. It is imperative to study the behavioural pattern of people in Ganjam district regarding their occupation, distribution of workforce, employment, wage structure, education, health, trend of agriculture production, land utilization pattern, landholding, irrigation potential, utilization capacities of fertilizer, industrial scenario, transport and communication, power, financial facilities through different banks and non-institutional agencies in general and with regard to fishermen of the district in particular.

District Profile

The district of Ganjam was formed on 1st April 1936. The meaning of the word "Ganjam" means "Ganj-I-am" which means "Granary of the world". The district has three sub-divisions, namely Chatrapur, Berhampur, and Bhanjanagar with 22 Blocks.

Location

The district of Ganjam in the State of Orissa is surrounded by Boudh-Kandhamal district of Orissa in the north, Srikakulam district of the Andhra Pradesh and Gajapati district of Orissa in the South, Bay of Bengal and Puri district in the east. This district lies between 19° to

20°-17′ of the northern latitude and 84°-6′ to 85°-11′ of eastern longitude.

Area of the District

The total area of the district is 8,206 square Km having three Sub-divisions and 22 blocks, 3212 villages, 19 towns, 14 Thasils, one municipality, 17 Notified Area Councils, 475 Gram Panchayats, 29 Police Stations, 12 Fire Stations and 12 Assembly Constituencies.

Climate

The climate of the Ganjam district is characterised by homogeneous temperature throughout the year. Humidity is very high. The maximum and minimum temperature recorded during the past five years was 31.50° and 23.70° Celsius respectively.

Rainfall

The average rainfall of the district is 129.56 cm per annum and with the onset of monsoon rain occurs between second week of June to early October. This rainfall is not sufficient for growing crops in the district. In the year 2004 the actual rainfall of the district recorded was 979.4 mm.

Type of Soil

The geographical locations in the district are alluvial, barren land late rite, Gondaaries, Cuddapah, Archum-comprising, ingenious, metamorphic rocks of Sedimentary origin. The soil can be divided into following parts.

1. *Alluvial:* Eastern part i.e. Coastal Belt.
2. *Late rite:* West hilly tableland with small patches of black button soil at the central part.
3. *Salty:* Clay, loamy, sandy-loan, soils are found towards Northeast coast i.e. Chilika area.

Administrative Set up

The administrative setup of the district mainly consists of sub-divisions, tahasils and blocks. This is depicted in Table 3.1.

Table 3.1. Sub-Divisions, Tahasils and Blocks of Ganjam District

Sl. No.	Sub-Division	Tahasils	Blocks
1.	Chatrapur	Chatrapur Khallikote Purusottampur Kodala Hinjilicut	Chatrapur Khallikote Purusottampur Kodala Hinjilicut Ganjam Polasara Kabisurya Nagar
2.	Berhampur	Berhampur Konisi Chikiti Digapahandi Patrapur	Rangeilunda Kukudakhandi Chikiti Patrapur
3.	Bhanjanagar	Ghumusar Buguda Aska Sorada	Bhanjanagar Belaguntha Jagannathprasad Buguda Aska Seragada Dharakote Sorada Digapahandi Sanakhemundi

Source: District at a Glance, 2001, Directorate of Economics and Statistics, Government of Orissa.

Table 3.1 reveals that there are three sub-division 14 Thasils and 22 Blocks in the district. The Sub-divsions are Berhampur, Chatrapur and Bhanjanagar.

Municipality and Notified Area Councils

The district has one municipality and 11 Notified Area Councils. They are as follows:

1. Municipality: Berhampur
2. Notified Area Councils

(*i*) Aska

(*ii*) Belaguntha

(*iii*) Bhanjanagar

(*iv*) Buguda

(*v*) Chatrapur

(*vi*) Chikiti

(*vii*) Digapahandi

(*viii*) Gopalpur

(*ix*) Ganjam

(*x*) Rambha

(*xi*) Hinjilicut.

Population

The total population of the State as per 2001 census is 3,67,06,920, which constitutes 3.57 per cent of the population of India. Table 3.2 exhibits the detail of population census for the year 1981, 1991 and 2001 of India, Orissa and the district of Ganjam.

The total population of Ganjam district has increased from 1981 to 2001 nearly 9.37 lakh i.e. 142.5 per cent whereas the India's rate of population increases up to 150.35 and the Orissa's population rate of increase is 139 per cent. So Ganjam's population growth rate is in little bit control than the population of India. The literacy rate of Ganjam has increased from 1981 to 2001 i.e. from 33.6 per cent to 62.94 per cent. It is a great achievement in literacy rate of Ganjam district in comparison to Orissa.

Occupational Distribution/Workforce

This district has a large work force of 13,05,932 persons in 2005. The occupational pattern of the workforce with percentage of total workers is given in Table 3.3.

Table 3.2. Population of India, Orissa State and Ganjam District as per Census 1981,1991, 2001 (in lakh)

Sl. No.	Classification	1981			1991			2001		
		India	Orissa	Ganjam	India	Orissa	Ganjam	India	Orissa	Ganjam
1.	Total Population	6833	263.7	22	8464	316.6	27.04	10270	367	31.37
2.	Population according to									
	(a) Sex				4390					
	Male	3530	133.1	11.15	407	160.6	13.4	5313	186	15.69
	Female	3303	130.6	11.52	0	156	13.56	4957	181	15.68
	Ratio	934	981	1033	927	971	1006	933	972	1000
	(b) Inhabitation				6288					
	Rural	5238	232.9	31.00	8217	274.25	22.80	7417	312	25.98
	Urban	1595	31.1	—	0	42.35	4.23	2854	55	5.38
	(c) Caste									
	SC	—	38.66	3.64	—	51.29	4.84	—	59	4.84
	ST	—	59.15	0.64	—	70.70	0.79	—	81	—
	Other	—	—	—	—	195	—	—	227	—
3.	Decadal Growth	24.66	20.2	16.6	23.9	20.1	19.25	21.3	15.9	16.01
4.	Density per km.	216	169	—	2.67	203	330	324	236	382
5.	Literacy Rate	43.6	33.6	33.6	52.2	49.1	46.7	65.4	63.6	62.94

Sources : 1. *Statistical Outline of Orissa*, Bureau of Statistics, Bhubaneswar, Orissa, 1995.
2. *Provisional Population Totals*, Orissa, 2001 series 22, Directorate of Census of Orissa.

Table 3.3. Occupational pattern of the Workforce in Ganjam District in 2005

Sl. No.	Category	No. of Workers	Percentage to total
1.	Cultivators	2,61,069	31.84
2.	Agricultural Labourers	1,71,651	20.94
3.	Household Industries (Including industries of manufacturing, processing, servicing & repairing etc.)	31,659	3.86
4.	Other Workers inncluding livestack, forestries plantation, mining, construction dairy and transport etc.	3,55,347	43.36
	Total	8,19,726	100
5.	Marginal Workers	4,86,206	37.23
	Total	13,05,932	100

Source: Statistical Abstract of Orissa, 2005, pp.15-19

Table 3.3 reveals that the cultivators of the district contribute 31.84 per cent of the total workforce of the district. The workforce on household industries is very less in the district, which contributes only 3.86 per cent of the total workers of the district whereas 20.94 per cent of agricultural labour is high to contribution of total workforce. There are 4,86,206 marginal workers in the district which contributes 37.23 per cent of total workers.

Agriculture

In this district, nearly 73.5 per cent of the total working force depend on agriculture for their livelihood. The principal crops of the district are paddy, ragi, black-gram, green-gram, til, groundnut, kolatha, sugarcane and chilly. rice is the single major crop of the district. It is cultivated in winter, autumn, and summer seasons. The production of different crops, yield rate is discussed Table 3.4.

Table 3.4. The Production of Major Crops in Ganjam District

(in '000 mt)

Sl. No.	Major Crops	1999-2000	2000-2001	2002-2003	2003-2004	2004-2005
1.	Rice	2,05,000	50,85,053	33,25,045	N.A	58,11,184
2.	Wheat	10,000	—	—		—
3.	Maize	11,930	7,193	6,077	7741	15,341
4.	Ragi	67,830	64,339	36,709	41,665	37,930
5.	Biri	13,830	9,895	12,073		14,544
6.	Kolatha	5,342	3,739	2,577		3,585
7.	Til	7,320	1,113	5,761		6,400
8.	Groundnut	52,516	61,265	42,021	56076	66,805
9.	Mustard	65,000	39	9	44	27
10.	Potato	16,020	16,370	12,969	16195	11,792
11.	Jute	—	—	—		—
12.	Mung	1,687	55,121	52,258		91,362
13.	Sugarcane	87,623	16,59,643	8,50,078	1362880	19,94,340

Sources: District Statistical Hand Book, Ganjam, 2005, pp. 21-23.

Table 3.4 shows that the production of rice is the highest i.e, 58,11,184,000 mt in 2004-05 against the production of sugarcane, ragi, mustard and groundnut. The production of mustard 27,000 mt in 2004-05 is the lowest i.e. 27,000 mt in the district.

Land Utilization Pattern

The land utilization pattern of the district up to the year 2005 is listed in Table 3.5. The forest area of the district is decreasing from year to year. The geogriphacial area, forest area, miscellaneous and other fallows remain the same in 2003-04 and 2004-05, but the net area sown has decreased by 9000 hectares.

Irrigation

Good irrigation system is linked with the production of crops. The irrigation system of the sample district is not up to the mark. The major project of the district is "Rushikulya irrigation system". The sourcewise irrigation potential of the district is shown in Table 5.6.

Table 3.5. Land Utilization Pattern in Ganjam District

(Area in '000 h)

Sl. No.	Land Utilization	1998-99	1999-2000	2003-04	2004-05
01.	Geographical area	8,070.6	8,777.6	871	871
02.	Forest area	3,149.9	3,15,000	3,15,000	3,15,000
03.	Miscellaneous (Crop and graves not included in net area sown)	29,000	2,999	22	22
04.	Permanent pasture and other gravings	25,000	24,000	11,000	20
05.	Land cultivable waste	11,000	11,000	20	11
06.	Land put to non-agricultural uses	45,000	45,000	60	60
07.	Barren and uncultivable land	47,000	47,000	37	37
08.	Current fallows	5,000	3,000	06	15
09.	Other fallows	8,000	8,000	11	11
10.	Net area sown sown	3,08,000	3,95,000	3,89,000	380,000

Source: Statistical Abstract of Orissa, 2005, pp. 40, 41.

I reveals that there is a change in major/medium irrigation project in the year 1993-94 to 2002-03. But the area has increased in the year 2002-03. Similarly the minor irrigation project (flow), has an increasing trend in the year 1994-95 and 2002-03.and 2004-05.

Fertilizers

Fertilizers play a vital role in increasing the productivity of the agricultural crops. The use of chemical fertilizer and organic manures in the district of Ganjam is not satisfactory. The consumption of chemical fertilizer from 2002-03 to 2004-05 in the district is shown in Table 3.7.

Table 3.6. Irrigation Potential of Ganjam District

(area in hectares)

Source-wise irrigation potential	1993-94	1994-95	1998-99	1999-2000	2000-01	2002-03	2004-05
Major/medium irrigation projects							
Kharif	1,02,584	1,08,970	1,70,000	1,19,930	1,22,810	1,25,060	12,808
Rabi	5,684	8,130	8,130	8,130	8,930	11,680	1,368
Total	1,08,268	1,17,100	1,78,130	1,28,060	1,31,740	1,36,740	1,4176
Minor irrigation projects (flow)							
Kharif	93,149	93,881	96,930	97,120	97,890	98,730	102,300
Rabi	6,378	6,494	6,800	6,800	6,800	6,800	6,800
Total	99,527	1,00,375	1,03,730	1,03,920	1,04,690	1,05,530	109,100
Minor irrigation projects (lift)							
Kharif	19,036	19,734	22,940	23,020	23,130	23,300	23,860
Rabi	11,422	11,841	13,770	11,620	13,880	13,980	14,320
Total	30,458	31,575	36,710	34,640	37,010	37,280	38,180

Source: District Statistical Hand Book, Ganjam, 2005, p.22.

Table 3.7. Consumption of Chemical Fertilizer in Ganjam District (2002-03–2004-05)

(in '000 mt)

Name of chemical fertilizer	2002-03	2003-04	2004-05
Nitrogenous (N)	21,610	27,860	32,120
Phosphate (P)	4,540	4,730	5,510
Potassium (K)	4,550	4,060	4,960
Total	30,700	36,650	42,590

Source: Economic Survey, Government of Orissa, 2005-06, Anx-20

The above table reveals that the chemical fertilizers, used by the cultivators of the district were 30,700 mt in 2002-03 which increase to 36,650 mt during the year 2003-04 and further enhanced to 42,590 mt in the year 2004-05. Mostly Nitrogenous is used and the least amount of use is Potassium.

Cooperative Societies and Loans

The main aim of the cooperatives is to save the rural poor, from the clutches of the landlords, sahukars 9331.25 etc, In the State of Orissa, the credit disbursement is undertaken by Orissa State Cooperative Banks, which finance the agricultural and non-agricultural sectors, to uplift the rural poor of the district as well as the State. The growth and development of the cooperative societies of the district is shown in Table 3.8. Agriculture cooperative societies have been decreasing while the non-agricultural cooperative societies have increased.

Loans advances have decreased from 9331.21 lakh in 2003-04 to 8980.25 lakhs in 2004-05. But in case of non-agricultureal credit cooperative societies loan advances have increased from 1516.36 lakh in 2003-04 to 1559.11 in 2004-05.

Table 3.8. Agricultural and Non-agricultural Credit Co-operative Societies of Ganjam District

(Rs in 'lakhs)

Year	Particular	No. of societies	Member	Working capital	Loan advanced
2003-04	Agricultural credit co-operative societies	402	269,532	18528.63	9331.25
	Non-agricultural credit co-operative societies	70	30,879	5872.10	1516.36
2004-05	Agricultural credit co-operative societies	401	2,80,312	19382.18	8980.25
2004-05	Non-agricultural credit co-operative societies	70	31,656	6,093.30	1589.11

Souce: District Statistical Hand Book, Ganjam, pp. 26,27.

Table 3.8 states that branches of agricultural credit co-operative societies have decreased. But Non-agricultural credit co-operative societies have remain the same. But working capital and members have increased in agricultural credit co-operative societies. Loans advanced decreased from 9331.25 lakh in 2003-04 to 8980.25 lakhs in 2004-05. But in case of Non-agricultural credit cooperative societies loans advanced have increased from 1516.36 lakh in 2003-04 to 1589.11 in 2004-05 and members of also increased from 30,879 in 2003-04 to 31,656 in 2004-05.

Forest Resources

Forest plays an important role in pollution control and environmental protection. They also reduce natural calamities like drought and floods. Forest is also considered to be an important source of livelihood for the tribal people of the district. The district has rich forest resources covering vast areas such as Sorada, Kodala, Khallikote, Buguda, Tarasingi, and Gallery etc. The main forest products of the district are timber, bamboo, mohua, tamarind, kenduleaves, salleaves, karange seeds, neem etc. The divisionwise classification of the forests in the district of Ganjam as on 1st April, 1996 are explained in Table 3.9.

Table 3.9. Classification of forest area by Legal Status in Ganjam District as on 31-3-2004 (area in sq. kms)

1. Reserve Forest	1485.69
2. Demarcated Projected Forest (DPF)	143.54
3. Undemarcated Project Forest (UDPF)	1167.36
4. Unclassified Forest	0.86
5. Other Forests under the control of Revenue Department	352.45
Total	3149.90

Source: Statistical Abstract of Orissa, 2005, p. 73.

The forest division of the Ganjam district has been divided into Ghumusar north and Ghumusar south. The total forest area of the district comes to 3149.90 sq. km as on 31st December 1999 (Table 3.9). The reserve forest area is 1485.69 sq. km., demarcated project forest area is 143.54 sq. km while undemarcated project forest area is 1167.36 sq. km. and unclassified forest area and area under the control of revenue department is 0.86 sq. km. and 352.45 sq. km respectively.

Livestock Resources

Animal resources plays an important role in rural development. The animal husbandry is the most important income generating activity of the district after agricultural production. Table 3.10 reveals that the numbers of buffalous are the highest in the district and ducks are the lowest in number as in September 2000. Proper care is highly essential for the growth and development of different animals in the district.

For this purpose, the role of veterinary hospitals and medical personnel are taken into account which is shown in Table 3.11.

Table 3.10. Livesstock and Animal Husbandry in Ganjam District (2000)

(in no)

Sl. No.	Category	Total livestock
1.	Cattle	8,41,661
2.	Buffaloes	9,72,966
3.	Sheep	1,45,914
4.	Goats	2,18,370
5.	Pigs	13,571
6.	Dogs	N.A.
7.	Fowls	14,27,292
8.	Duck	6,450
9.	Other livestock	3,747

Source: Statistical Abstract of Orissa, 2005, pp. 77-79.

Table 3.11 reveals that the veterinary hospitals and dispensaries have not shown any increasing trend in the years 1995–96 and 2000-01, but increase in 2003-04 remain the same in 2004-05. The livestock inspectors show an increasing trend in all these four years (i.e, 1992–93 to 1995–96). The number of A.I. centres is reduced to 98, but again in the year 2003-04 it has increased to 154 and remain the same during the year 2004-05.

Power

Now-a-days power is considered to be the most important factor for economic growth of the people. The constant flow of power and the utilisation is also taken as essential part of the district. Due to reforms in power set-up, the Orissa Hydro Electricity Board has been renamed and two new corporations named first one Grid Corporation of Orissa and the second one is Orissa Hydro Power Corporation came

Table 3.11. The Number of Veterinary Institutions and Personnel in Ganjam District

(In nos.)

Sl. No.	Veterinary Institutions	1992-93	1993-04	1994-95	1995-96	2000-01	2003-04	2004-05
1.	Veterinary Hospitals and Dispensaries	37	37	39	37	37	39	39
2.	Veterinary Assistants Surgeon	59	59	61	50	—	44	45
3.	L.A. Centres	233	235	243	236	—	245	245
4.	Livestock Inspector	270	272	283	329	—	243	245
5.	A.I. Centres	83	85	86	106	98	154	154
6.	Normal Livestock aid centres	—	—	—	144	—	—	—

Source: Statistical Abstract of Orissa, 2005, p. 80
Statistical Hand Book of Ganjam, 2005, p. 35.

into existence on 1st November 1997. Now there are four power companies namely:

1. Central Electricity Supply Company of Orissa Ltd., (CESCO).
2. North-Eastern Electricity Supply Company of Orissa Ltd., (NESCO).
3. Western Electricity Supply Company of Orissa Ltd., (WESCO).
4. Southern Electricity Supply Company of Orissa Ltd., (SESCO).

Table 3.12. Division-wise Consumption of Electricity in Ganjam District

(In million units)

Sl. No.	Consumption Pattern	G.N.E.D. Ganjam	I.B.E.D. Berham-pur	B.N.E.D. Bhanja-nagar
1.	Domestic	73.74	90.453	59.46
2.	Kutira Joti	57.09	26.530	1.595
3.	Commercial	7.427	7.759	8.129
4.	Commercial over 10 km	1.984	5.037	1.306
5.	Small Industries	6.544	6.818	7.098.
6.	Medium Industries	3.795	4.007	2.504
7.	Large Industries	34.131	1.220	2.777
8.	General Purpose	6.190	2.457	0.000
9.	Heavy Industries	0.000	0.000	0.000
10.	Power Inclusive Industries	44.670	0.000	0.000.
11.	Public Lighting	0.626	1.867	1 .832
12.	Railway Traction	0.000	0.000	0.000
13.	Irrigation	6.621	3.604	9.947
14.	Public Waterworks	6.986	1.287	0.849
15.	Bulk Supply, domestic	0.330	0.000	0.807
16.	Public Institution	2.456	4.847	0.735
	Total	252.590	155.986	97.039

Source: District Statistical Hand Book, Ganjam, 1999, p. 62.

The area of operation of Southern Electricity Supply Company of Orissa Ltd. is the district of Ganjam, Gajapati, Boudh, Kandhmal, Nabarangapur, Koraput, Rayagada and Malkanagiri. The divisionwise use of electricity in the district of Ganjam is explained in Table 3.12.

It is found from Table 3.12 that G.N.E.D. Ganjam consumes the highest power of 252.590 million units while I.B.E.D. Berhampur consumed 155.986 million units while B.N.E.D. Bhanjanagar consumed the lowest i.e, 97.039 million units. highest consumption of electricity is found for domestic purpose.

Transport

Good infrastructure facilities are highly essential for the economic development of the district. Transport is a basic infrastructure which needs due consideration for the economic development of the district. Proper transport system is highly essential for marketing of the agricultural and products of the district in the district there are three modes of transport, i.e. Roadways, Railways and Waterways. The different types of roads and railways are explained in which shows a phenomenal growth in all type of transport. Table 3.93.

Table 3.13 reveals that there is no increase in National Highways. But the State Highways, has decreased in the year 2003-04 but village roads show an increasing trend in year 2003-04. In 2001- 02 the trend of National Highways increased to 205 kilometres where the State Highways, major district roads have decreased. It almost remain the same In the year 2003-3004. The list of registered vehicles of the district is illustrated in Table 3.14.

Table 3.14 reveals that the number of motorcycles, scooters and mopeds have increased tremendously. Two, wheelers were 2840 during the year 1992-93 but increased to 58,206 at the end of the 1998-99. Similarly registered trucks and lorries were 57 in 1992-93, but increased to 2735 at the end of the year 1998-99. In the year 2004-05 there is tremendous increase in different vehicles. In comparison to 2003-04, the total vehicles increased to

132,085 in the year 2004-05. From the table it is clear that there is a phenomenal growth in all types of vehicle.

Table 3.13. Length of Different Categories of Roads and Railways Route in the District of Ganjam in the Year 2003-04

(in km)

Sl. No.	Categories of Roads	1995-96	1996-97	1999-2000	2000-01	2001-02	2003-04
1.	National Highways	87	87	87	87	205	212
2.	Express Highways	—	—		—	—	—
3.	State Highways	525	525	669	770	623	623
4.	Major District Roads	303	303	158	158	92	92
5.	Other district Roads	430	452	452	487	497	481
6.	Classified Villages Roads	200	200	200	200	200	—
7.	Villages Roads	1,351	1,397	2,146	2,118	2,138	2.338
8.	Grama Panchayat Roads	6,717	6,717	6,717	6,717	6,717	6,717
9.	Panchayat Samiti Roads	761	761	12	761	761	761
10.	Forest Roads	480	480	480	480	480	480
11.	Municipal/NAC Roads	—	—	4,812	1,100	—	—
	Total	10,854	10,922	15,733	12,878	11,713	—
12.	Railway route Length	—		80	86	86	—
13.	No. of Railway Stations	—	—	11	11	11	—

Source: Statistical Abstract of Orissa, 2005, pp. 105, 106.

Communication

Communications is another important infrastructure requisite for the rapid economic growth and development of the district. Telecommunication, Telegraphs, Postal services helps in transmitting the messages from one corner to another. It helps in communicating various facts and information among the people of the district. The total number of communication infrastructure of the district is presented in Table 3.15.

Table 3.14. Number of Motor Vehicles, Registered in the District Ganjam as on 2003-04.

Sl. No.	Vehicles	1994-95	1996-97	1997-98	1998-99	2002-03	2003-04	2004-05
1.	Motorcycle, Scooters and Mopeds	40,701	48,564	—	58,206	92,333	103502	114509
2.	Three-Wheelers, Auto-Rickshaws	440	553	651	860	1804	2033	2263
3.	Jeep and station wagons	1,151	1221	230	1,275	1424	1446	1451
4.	Private Cars	984	1,037	1,118	1,240	2343	2571	2878
5.	Taxis	171	183	204	235	413	477	560
6.	Contract Carriages	135	155	168	184	197	197	197
7.	State Carriages	476	533	566	612	730	791	853
8.	Trucks and Lorries	2,32	2.477	2,585	2:735	3681	4260	4810
9.	Petrol and water carries	24	—	—	—	NA	NA	—
10.	Tractor And Trawlers	869	1,321	1,546	1,731	2812	3350	3891
11.	Miscellaneous Vehicles	169	305	381	401	559	623	673
	Total	47,452	56,339	61,078	67,479	1,06,296	119250	132085

Source : Statistical Abstract of Orissa, 2005, pp. 108, 109.

Table 3.15. Number of Post Offices, Telephone Exchanges and Telephone Connections in Ganjam district as on 31-3-2005

Sl. No.	Categories	2003-04	2004-05
1.	Head Post Offices	4	4
2	Sub-Post Offices	117	117
3.	Branch Post Offices	555	555
	Total Post Offices	676	676
4.	Telegraphic facilities combined offices	372	372
5.	Total Telephone exchange	82	82
6.	Exchange Capacity	22,086	22,086
7.	Wiring connections	30,624	30,624
8.	No. of PBX connected to the exchange	05	05

Source: Statistical Abstract of Orissa, 2005, P-107

Table 3.15 reveals that the total post offices of the district are 676 as on 31-03-2005. There are 82 telephone exchanges and 5 Private Branch Exchange (PBX) in the district. In the year 2004-2005 there is no change from the previous year 2003-04.

Industrial Scenario

The district has rich mineral resources but the industrial scenario of the district is not attractive due to improper infrastructural facilities. The district has only 3 big industries namely. Sugar Industry at Aska, Indian Rare Earth Ltd. near Chatrapur and Jayashree Chemicals at Ganjam. The district has 5521 small scale industries (SSIs) with an investment of Rs. 9,115.87 lakh and providing employment opportunity for 27,543 persons as on 31 March, 1999. The number of SSI units, investment of employment opportunities is illustrated in Table 3.16.

Table 3.16 shows an upswing trend, but during the year 2003-04 the units have decrease from 331 to 313 units. Employment opportunities have also been increased. From 1050 in 2002-03 to 1377 in 2003-04. Total capital investment has also increased from 105,031 lakh in 2002-03 to 1329.551akh in 2003-04.

Table 3.16. Number of Industries, Total Employees, Production Capital and Net Value

Year	No. of SSI units established	Total Capital Investment (Rs. in lakh)	Employment generated (No.)
1998-1999	224	1752.08	1472
1999-2000	234	1762.56	1517
2000-2001	321	619.89	1118
2001-2002	328	1078.06	1233
2002-2003	331	1050.31	1050
2003-3004	313	1329.55	1377

Source : Statistical Abstract of Orissa, 2005, pp. 87-89.

Market

For economic growth of an area, appropriate marketing facility is highly essential. Two types of markets are found in the district. They are:

1. Primary or daily market and
2. Secondary or weekly market (heat)

The main market places are in Berhampur, Hinjilikatu, Aska, Bhanjanagar, Kabisurjyanagar, Bellaguntha, Buguda, Kodala, and Sorada. The important agricultural products dealt in the market are paddy, rice, blackgram, greengram, groundnut and different oil seeds. In the weekly market or haat, the buyers and sellers meet together in a central place, once in a week to sell and buy their products. The important weekly markets, of the district are in Berhampur, Hinjilikatu, Bellaguntha, Kamsi and Huma. Huma is famous for dry fish. The buyers and sellers from different parts of Orissa, also from Andhra Pradesh and West Bengal come to sell and buy the dry fish at Huma. Similarly the Hinjilkatu weekly market is famous for cattle and Bellaguntha is famous for grass products. The main export products of the district are Pattasarees, Panmasala, tobacco. Silver products, dry fish, forest products and agricultural products.

Education

Education plays an important role for the socio-economic development of the nation. A nation remains incomplete without development of human resources. For the development of the human resources education plays a vital role. In this present scenario to meet the challenges from every corner, education cannot be ignored. It is the duty of the Government to provide minimum education to the children of the nation. Besides general education institutions, the district has two industrial training institutions, i.e. one is Berhampur and another is at Kabisuryanagar.

Berhampur is the centre for education. There are Engineering Schools, schools for diploma in nursing, schools for fisheries, engineering colleges etc. There is one industrial training school in berhampur. All the technical schools, from Diploma to Degree levels are established in and around Berhampur. The progress of the education from primary school to college level is explained in the Table 3.17.

Table 3.17. Progress of the Education in Ganjam district 2003-04

(in no)

Institutions	No. of Schools	Enrolment	No. of Teachers
Primary School	2,936	4,51,522	5,665
Secondary School	443	9,0150	4,011
Middle School	642	80,094	4,437
General College	No. of Govt. Colleges	No. of Added Colleges	
NA	10	33	

Source: Statistical Abstract of Orissa, 2005, p. 112-122.

Table 3.17 reveals the position of primary schools; secondary schools, middle schools and Colleges along with student enrolment position and number of teachers. There are 2936 primary schools with an enrolment of 4,51,522 students and there are 5665 teachers similarly there are 443 secondary schools with an enrolment of 90,150 and there are 4011 teachers. There are also 642 middle schools with an enrolment of 80094 students and 4437 teachers are working in the students in the district there are 10 Government colleges and 33 aided colleges.

Health Services

"Health is Wealth", a well designed. Health service is essential for human development. For sound health one should have good food, water, good sanitation, proper housing, education, and good environment. According to the National Health Policy "Health for All" and mostly to the rural and the tribal people is essential. The number of health institutions of the district along with other information are shown Table 3.18.

Table 3.18. Number of Alloptahic, Homoeopathic and Ayurvadic institutions (2004-05)

(in no)

Medical colleges/District Headquarters hospitals	02
Sub-divisional or Other Hospitals	11
Community Health Centres	19
Primary Health Centres	83
Primary Health Centres (Mobile Health Units)	707
Beds in Hospital (2003-04)	1541
Ayurvedic Hospitals & Dispensary	49
Homoeopathic Hospitals or Dispensaries	44

Source : Statistical Abstract of Orissa, 2005, pp. 123-126.

Table 3.18 reveals the total picture of medical setup of the district. Allopathic is in demand in comparison to

Homoepathic and Ayurvedic. There are 2 medical colleges, 11 Sub Divisional Hospitals, 19 Community Health Centres, 83 Primary Health Centres, 49 Ayurvedic Hospitals and 44 Homoeopathic hospitals or dispensaryies. Total number of beds available in the hospital is 1541.

Financial Institutions

The role of financial institutions is more important in our country. This will help the economic growth of the country as well as the district. The proper network of the financial institutions will help the rural poor for their upliftment of the living standard. The district has co-operative banks, Regional Rural Banks (RRBs) and Commercial Banks (CBs) as well as other private sector banks. Table 3.19 explains the deposits and credit of commercial bank.

Table 3.19 reveals that as on 31-3-2004 there are 127 public sector banks accumulating a deposit of Rs.1634,00 lakh and disposes Rs. 56,500 lakh. Similarly RRBs, have 64 branches which have accumulated a deposit of Rs. 30,800 lakh and disbursed a loan of Rs. 14,300 lakh. The commercial banks in the district have 191 branches with aggregate deposit of Rs. 94,200 lakh and produced a loan of Rs. 70,700 lakh.

Non-Banking Financial Institutions

Besides the Commercial Banks, Co-operative and Regional Rural Banks (RRBs), there are 13 Non-Banking Financial Corporations (NBFCs), functioning in the State. They are playing an important role in the flow of resources into the State economy. These NBFCs include the Orissa State Financial Corporation (OSFC), a branch of Unit Trust of India (UTI), small Scale Industrial Development Bank of India (SIDBI). These financial institutions plays an active role for financial transaction and growth in the district.

National Bank for Agricultural and Rural Development (NABARD)

As per the recommendation of the Committee to Review Arrangements for Institutional Credit for Agricultural and

Table 3.19. Aggregate Deposit and Bank Credits of Scheduled Commercial Banks in the District of Ganjam as on 31-3-2004.

(Rs. in lakhs)

Sl. No.	Items	1996	Mrch 1997	Mrch 1998	Mrch 2000	Mrch 2004
1.	Public sector banks					
	Reporting Offices	127	127	122	188	127
	Deposits (Rs. in Lakhs)	4,76.70	6,02.87	6,80.57	14,38.43	16,3400
	Credit (Rs. in Lakhs)	89.54	2,00.64	2,26.01	4,41.90	56,500
2.	Regional Rural Banks					
	Reporting Offices	61	61	62	65	64
	Deposits (Rs. in Lakhs)	42.60	42.60	93.87	15.617	30,800
	Credit (Rs. in Lakhs)	26.54	26.54	43.77	6,018	4,14,300
3.	All Scheduled Commercial Banks					
	Number of Offices	199	189	185	199	191
	Deposits (Rs. in Lakhs)	5,27.60	6,57.76	7,29.21	12,06.50	1,94,200
	Credit (Rs. in Lakhs)	2,16.88	2,28.04	2,73.30	3,62.35	70,700

Source : Statistical Abstract of Orissa, 2005, pp. 191-192.

Rural Development (CRAFICARD), the Government of India enacted the National Bank for Agricultural and Rural Development Act, in 1992. Accordingly, NABARD was set up in and started functioning as an Apex Rural Bank with a view to provide credit for agriculture, Small-Scale Industries, village industries and development of rural infrastructure. A regional office is working at Bhubaneswar. It is providing refinance support through co-operatives and RRBs for channellising the funds to priority sectors in rural areas.

Insurance

Life Insurance Corporation (LIC) of India is the only authorized institution to take up insurance business. It collects funds from general public through various schemes, and utilize the amount towards the development of social-oriented sectors like power, drinking water and other basic infrastructural amenities. The head office of LIC is at Mumbai. It is operating throughout India under seven zones. The State of Orissa comes under eastern zone. In the State, three divisional offices are functioning at Cuttack, Berhampur and Sambalpur. Under the division office of Berhampur 14 branches are functioning. Ganjam district has six branches. They are Bhanjanagar, Berhampur Church Road Branch-1, Aska Road -2, Aska, Career Agent Branch (CAB) at Bijipur and Chatrapur. There are also other insurance companies. They are:

1. The New India Insurance Co.Ltd.
2. The National Insurance Comp. Ltd
3. The Oriental Insurance Co. Ltd
4. The United India Insurance Co. Ltd.

These institutions undertake agreement to protect the public property which is exposed to a variety of physical hazards against a nominal payment called premium.

Fishing Activities in Ganjam

Ganjam, one of the coastal districts of Orissa has 3171 villages. The population of the district is 31,36,937, out of which fishermen population is 1,31,192 as per 2001 census. The fishing area of the district is 9449.045 hectares and the district has a coastline of 60Km. The fishery activity is divided into two typesmarine fishing and inland fishing.

Marine Fishing in Ganjam District

The majority of fishermen communities are migrants from Andhra Pradesh and settled here for centuries and speak Telugu. The dialect used by the fishermen community is a combination of Oriya-Telugu language. The migration can be traced back to the 16th century when Basudev Mangaraj, the ruler of 'machagar' invited them to settle at the mouth of River Devi, district of Puri and on the Coast of Ganjam to protect him from sea pirates.

Fishing is carried out by Telugu fishermen called Noliyas and Oriya fishermen called 'Keutas'. 'Noliya's are further divided into 'Jalaries' and 'Vodabalijas'. The Jalaries are furthur sub-divided into Edu Ratla Group and Pennendu Ratla Group. The castes of native fisherfolk include Nilari, Keuta or Korada and Gokha. The Noliya's constitute 59 per cent, Kondra16 per cent, Keuta 10 per cent, Kantla 9 per cent, and Sondi 6 per cent of the total marine population. The Noliya's fishing in the sea are not declared as scheduled caste. They are accorded as OBC (other backward caste). The detail discussion about the five sub-castes are as follows:

(a) *Noliya or 'Jolari'* : The Noliya's again are sub-divided into Aduratla and Pannendu Ratla castes. They form 59 per cent of total marine population. They go into the off-shore fishing and women folk engage themselves in marketing of fish and allied activities such as curing, drying of fish etc.

(b) *Kondra* : They from 16 per cent of the total population. They usually are craft and gear owners and act as middlemen in fish trade.

(c) *Sondi* : The Sondi's usually are wine sellers who in recent times are engaged in money-lending and allied fishing activities. They form six per cent of the total population.

(d) *Keuta* : They form about 10 per cent of the population and are known as 'Kaibarta'. They engage in fishing using traps which is considered a lower caste activity.

(e) *Karatia* : They are around nine per cent of the total population. They use bamboo traps called beja and menjha which are lowered into water after scattering fish feed all over it.

Habitation

The main streets of the villages are occupied by well to do fisher folk like middlemen, owners of boats and nets and money-lenders. Their houses are made of brick walls and asbesto roofs. The poor fishermen have houses made of mud walls, thatched with palm leaves. Generally they have small backyard with few plants and one or two coconut trees. Cooking on religious occasions and social functions are done on community ovens arranged in the middle of each street. Every house has a outer verandah (arugu) where all nets and gears are kept and fish are salted and dried.

Population

The total marine population of the district are depicted in Table 3.20.

Table 3.20. Total Marine Population of Ganjam District

No. of Village	No. of House = holds	Fishermen population			
		Male	Female	Children	Total
28	7,325	9,709	9,032	18,765	37,506

Source: Assistant Director of Fisheries, Marine, Ganjam

Table 3.20 shows that nearly 25 per cent fishermen are male. The number of villages are 28 and total marine fishermen population is 37,506.

Religious Festivals

Lord Narsimha of Simanchalam, Lord Vishnu of Tirupati and Lord Jagannath of Puri are popular Gods among the community, but there are the local Goddesses that plays an important role in the day to day life of the fisher folk. They practise their ancestral called *Gangamma* (the water Goddess). She is worshipped throughout the coast by all fisher folk. Apart from them "*Ammavaru*", "*Poleramma*", are goddess who are worshipped with various names. An important aspect of festival is *Kothammavasya* (Telugu New year day), *Mahasankranthi, Kartika Poornima* and *Bahuda* Yatra. They sacrifice small birds like cocks and animals like *goats, sheep* etc. to the mother Goddess. A wide variety of fruits, coconuts, camphor, incense sticks and flowers are offered to the sea Goddesses and elaborate prayers are performed for ensuring the safe return of men folk from sea with a good catch.

Crafts and Gears

The various types of crafts operating are *catamarans, teppas, padhua,* and *nava.* The common gears used are *jago, kilumala, kavala, kaata, irgali, marala, mala, khepa* and *netthala vala.* Similarly different types of nets are used. Costliest nets are *nettala,* and the cheapest one is *disco net.* The longevity and costs are directly co-related. Nearly six types of nets known as "*valas*" in local language are used in these villages. The assetless persons are at. the bottom of the ladder of the community.

Fishing Activities

The activities of fishermen in the district are full time fishermen - 6886, while part time fishermen are 527, occasional fishermen are 208 and fishermen engaged in anciliary activities are 5746.

Health

The fishermen in the sample district are found to maintain a sound physique. But most of the fishermen are suffering from water-born diseases like warm infection, cholera, typhoid, diarrhoea, malnutrition etc. Death during delivery has also affected to a large extent. They also live in unhygienic conditions. Health service is not provided to a great extent. They depend on local '*vaidyas*' for treatment. They believe that their health deteriorates only due to bad spiritual action or black magic. Family planning is also gaining momentum in the district. The infant mortality rate is quiet high. When they are in serious conditions they go for allopathic treatment available at the dispensaries and public health centres. In critical cases they prefer to visit private doctors in Berhampur city for quick recovery and good treatment. All the sample villages have safe drinking water facility. They use tube-well water for drinking. But they bath in the contaminated water in the open tanks and ponds.

Education

Education is mostly neglected in this district and it is the cause of various social evils in the society. An interesting finding in this district is that percentage of girls in the primary and secondary schools is higher than the boys because the later prefers to use their time in learning the techniques of fishing rather than in learning alphabets in the schools. It was also interesting to note that after the implementation of mid-day meal programme, free books and dresses for girls in the primary level, the students attendance in the school has increased. Most of the fishermen families send their children to schools to have a square meal in the school, which will save the food for other members of the family. Also some NGO's like UAA in Ganjam Block and PREM in Gopalpur have taken up project for primary education of the Noliya's in the District.

Food

The pattern of food differs from peak period to lean periods. The Noliya's consume stale rice and *raggie* spice early in the morning, before going for fishing operation. They also carry lunch with them. They mostly depend on raggie and coarse for the basic food and fish fry as curry. Vegetables are rarely used for curry. During the peak period they also consume eggs and meat.

Role of Women and Children

The fishermen of these villages live in a nuclear family referred to as '*kutumbam*' with patriarchal authority. The primogeniture is reflected both in property inheritance and in functions, irrespective of boy or girl child. The management of income, marketing of fish and household management is done by the mother, daughters and daughter-in-law. Fish smoking, salting, drying working in plantations, working as manual labour, and agricultural activities such as sowing and transplanting in fields, labour and working as maid servants is done by the fisherwomen.

The decisions regarding savings, acquisition of jewels, purchasing of assets, education and marriage of children are all taken up by women. In spite of her multifarious duties, the mother in the family does not delegate any of her important role in management and finance to other female members in the family. The authority pattern between the head of the family and his wife is highly flexible, democratic and balanced depending upon the area of decision-making. The fishermen community express a distinct preference for male child as they believe that, the more sons, the more heads and hands will take up fishing enterprise and increase household income. The lower strata fishermen children idle away their time till 15 years after which they join the family enterprises. The fishermen of upper strata educate their girls. The children of these households imparted education so that they can go for salaried jobs. Mostly the girl children work at home or go for wage. The unmarried sons and daughter-in-laws have little say in the household management. Sometimes the married sons participate in decision-making which include purchase of crafts and gears or house constructions. Girls have no stake in the family property.

Environment

The fishermen of the district are concerned about depletion of fishery resources in the sea. They feel that, depletion of fishery resources is occurring due to over fishing by mechanized boats and rest due to destructive gears. This has effected in decrease of prawn, seed, black pamphlets, Shark's, Jew fish, Silver Bellies, fins, Bombay duck etc. They believe that rough seas and cyclones etc. are to be blamed.

Electricity

All the villages are connected with electricity but only those fishermen who have good economic conditions and *pucca* houses have made use of it. Entertainment is a rarity in these villages. Very few people afford to have a television set.

The infrastructure facilities in the marine sector are discussed below:

Fish Landing Centre

The fish landing centre of the district are shown in Table 3.21.

Table 3.21. Fish Landing Centres of Ganjam District

Sl. No.	Block	Fish landing centre
1	Ganjam	Prayagi, Kantigarh, Gokharikuda, Rushikulya base.
2.	Chatrapur	Nolia N. Gaon, Sana Aryapalli, Bada Aryapalli.
3.	Rangailunda	Gopalpur, Rev Katuru, New Boxipalli, New Golabandha.
4.	Chikiti	Patisonapur, Sonepur, Rameyapatna and Markandi.

Source: Compiled by the author.

Fishery Jetties

There are three fishery Jetties in Ganjam district. They are Pathara Jetty, Palur Jetty and Sabalia Jetty.

Fishing Harbour

A fair weather light range port has been set up at Gopalpur-on-sea to facilitate trade of the district. This port at Gopalpur has started in the year 1990-91 at a project cost of 805.30 lakh and completed in the year 1993-94.

Fish Landing Platform

There is one fish-landing platform at Rusukulya FLC which was started in the year 1992-93 and completed in 1993-94 at a projected cost of Rs. 9.4 lakh.

Inland Fisheries

Ganjam district is considered to be one of the potential aquaculture resources districts of the State in the form of freshwater, brackish water and marine fisheries. In Ganjam district there are plenty of resources for pond culture, reservoir fisheries and shrimp culture. These resources provide an excellent opportunity to develop pisciculture for increasing fish production to meet the growing demand of the people as well as play an important role for providing employment opportunity to the rural people. It is depicted in Table 3.22.

Table 3.22. Inland Fishermen's Population as Per Census 2001

No. of fishermen village	No. of House-hold	Male popula-tion	Female popula-tion	Children	Total
444	17,866	27,635	24,952	41,099	93,686

Sources: Collected from the report of Assistant Director Fisheries, Berhampur.

Table 3.22 reveals that the number of total inland fishermen of the district is 93,686, which is quiet higher than marine fishermen population. It also shows that there are 444 inland fishermen village. Number of households are 17,866.

Aquaculture Resources

The aquaculture resources of the district in different sectors are shown in Table 3.23.

Table 3.23. Aquaculture resources of Ganjam district

(Area in Hect.)

Sl. No.	Category of Resources	Water area Available		Water Area Utilized	
		No. of Tanks/ Ponds	Area (ha)	No. of Tanks/ Ponds	Area (ha)
1.	**Fresh water (Tank/Ponds)**				
	(*a*) Gram Panchayat	7504	8637.81	51.16	5068.98
	(*b*) Private	3324	2210.10	2613	1922.86
	Total	**10828**	**10847.91**	**7729**	**699.84**
2.	MIP/ Reservoir	246	5703.00	161	4169.00!
	Grand Total	11074	16550.91	7890	11160.84
3.	Brackish Water Resources	—	—	—	—
	(*a*) Government	—	3309.29	—	2522.08
	(*b*) Private	—	826.61	—	657.98
	Total	**—**	**4135.90**	**—**	**3180.06**

Source: Unpublished record of the District Fisheries office-cum-CEO, Berhampur.

Table 3.23, shows that the water spread area is 4135.90 ha, and the water utilized area is 3180.06 ha. It signifies that there is scope for aquaculture resource in inland sector. It includes brackish water resources of the Government and also private individual.

Major Activities

In order to increase spawn and fry production the following steps are being taken:

1. To develop incremental water area through FFDA to increase fish production.
2. To render training to pisciculture on modern scientific pisciculture.
3. To implement other government sponsored schemes.
4. To develop brackish water area for shrimp production.
5. To develop pisciculture in reservoir/minor irrigation plant through Self-helf Group and primary fishermen's co-operative society.

One of the major factors of success in pisciculture is to stock timely quality fish seed in farmer's ponds. To ensure the Department takes lion's share in shouldering the responsibility of fish seed production and supply to the farmers. The government has established seed producing farms in different sectors. The responsibility is shared by:

1. Departmental farms.
2. Orissa Pisciculture Development Corporation.
3. The Orissa State Fisheries Co-operative Federation.

Departmental Farms

The farms are located in different parts of the district. It is shown in Table 3.24.

Table 3.24. Location of Firms in Ganjam District.

(In hectare)

Sl. No.	Name of the farms	Location	Category of the farms	Total areas	Water area
1.	Digapahandi	Digapahandi	Breeding & rearing	17.81	11.63
2.	Sagarbandha	Berhampur	Rearing	16.64	4.83
3.	Dhobabandha	Berhampur	Rearing	4.16	2.80
4.	Aska	Aska	Rearing	4.94	1.42
5.	Pudamari	Pudamari	Rearing	5.31	3.70
			Total	48.86	24.38

Source: Unpublished record of District Fisheries Office-cum-CEO, Berhampur.

Table 3.24 indicates that five farms are operating in the district. Besides the above there are two other departmental farms namely Bhanjanagar and Mallad that are being managed by OPDC and Fish fed respectively for production of fish seed. Out of the five firms Digapahandi deals with breeding and rearing while other four firm deals with rearing only.

Spawn and Fry Production in Departmental Farms

The details of spawn and fry production in departmental firms for the year 2001-02 to 2005-06 are as shown in Table 3.25.

Table 3.25. Spawn and Fry Production in Ganjam District

(In lakhs)

Sl. No.	Year	Spawn Production in lakh		Fry production in lakh	
		Actual	Target	Actual	Target
1.	2001-02	220.00	221.00	56.00	55.00
2.	2002-03	220.00	223.00	72.02	55.00
3.	2003-04	270.00	350.00	126.50	110.00
4.	2004-05	500.00	540.00	163.22	130.00
5.	2005 as on Feb.06	550.00	520.00	184.00	130.00

Source: Unpublished record of District Fisheries office-cum-CEO, Berhmapur.

Table 3.25 shows that spawn and fry production is constantly increasing year after year. Spawn production has reached 550 lakh and fry production 184 lakh in the year 2006 from 220 and 56 lakh respectively in the year 2001-02.

Orissa Pisciculture Development Corporation (OPDC)

Apart from the Departmental farms the OPDC has also established a hatchery at Bhanjanagar which supplies fry to pisciculturist of the district. The spawn and fry production of the OPDC is depicted in Table-3.26.

Table 3.26. Spawn and Fry Production in OPDC form

Sl. No.	Particular	Achievement		
		During 2003-04	During 2004-05	During 2005-06
1.	Spawn production in crore	15.93	16.92	16.93
2.	Fry production in lakh	349.00	395.74	489.405

Source: Unpublished record of District Fisheries offlce-cum CEO, Berhampur.

Table 3.26 shows that spawn production during 2003-04 is 15.93 crore, in 2004-05 it has increased to 16.92 crore and in 2005-06 it has furthern increased to 16.93 crores. Similarly fry production has increased from 349 lakh in the year 2003-04 to 489.405 lakh in the year 2005-06.

The Orissa State Fisheries Co-operative Federation (Fishfed)

The Government fish farm Mallad is at present under the possession of the Fishfed. The federation has produced spawn and fry is shown in Table 3.27.

Table 3.27. Achievement of Fishfed in Ganjam District

(In lakh)

Sl. No.	Progress item	2003-04	2004-05	2005-06
1.	Spawn production	200.00	120.00	70.00
2.	Fry production	40.75	31.33	1780

Source: Unpublished record of District Fisheries officecum-CEO, Berhmapur.

Table 3.27 shows that Fishfed has shown a decline trend both in spawn production as well as fry production. The spawn production has decrease from 200 lakh in 2003-04 to 70 lakh in 2005-06. Similarly the fry production has also decreased from 40.75 lakh in 2003-04 to 17.80 lakh in 2005-06. It is gradually turning out to be a sick unit.

Private Firms

Besides Government Sector the private fanners have been encouraged to produce seed. The seed producing farms in the district are as shown in Table 3.28.

Table 3.28 shows the private farms of the district along with the name of entrepreneurs with water area utilized by them. This organization provide finance to these entrepreneurs, which is shown in Table 3.29.

Table 3.28. Private farms of Ganjam District

(in Acre)

Sl. No.	Name of the Entrepreneur	Water area available in	Water area utilized in	Remarks
1.	Sri Gopal Krushna Jenna, At- Siddhakhandi, Block-Digapahandi	6.00	6.00	Financed under KSK
2.	Sri Banamali Pradhan At-Kamalpy Block-K.0S. Nagar	19.50	19.50	FFDA development

Source: Unpublished record of District Fisheries office-cum-CEO, Berhmapur.

Table 3.29 shows there is an increase in spawn production from 695 lakh in 2004-05 to 740 lakh during the year 2005-06 but there is a fall in fry production 191.43 lakh in 2004-05 to 172.00 lakh in 2005-06.

Table 3.29 Spawn and Fry Production in Private Sector

(In lakh)

Sl. No.	Name of the Entrepreneur	2004-05		2005-06	
		Spawn produced	Fry produced	Spawn produced	Fry producede
1.	Sri Gopal Krushna Jenna, At- Siddhakhandi, Block-Digapahandi	310.00	83.43	330.00	70.00
2.	Sri Banamali Pradhari At-Kanialpur Block-K.S. Nagar	385.00	108.00	410.00	102.00
	Total	695.00	191.43	740.00	172.00

Source: Unpublished record of District fisheries office-cum-CEO, Berhmapur.

Fish Farmer Development Agency (FFDA)

For effective implementation and popularization of improved scientific method of pisciculture so as to increase fish production the FISH FARMERS DEVELOPMENT AGENCY' was established during the year 1976 under the Centrally-sponsored scheme. The main aims and objectives of the agency are as follows:

1. To develop water area through excavation/ renovation of private/ G.P. tanks for increasing fish production.
2. To prepare project report and coordinate the financing bank for institutional finance under subsidy scheme.
3. To arrange supply of quality fish and prawn seed to fanners.
4. To render technical guidance to fish fanners.
5. To organize short-term training for fish fanners for latest technical know how.
6. To promote employment opportunity through integrated fish farming. The details of a achievement of the agency is given in table-3.30.

Table 3.30. The Performance of FFDA in Ganjam District

(in hectare)

Sl. No.	Progress item	Achievement 2003-04		2004-05		2005-06	
		Target	Achievement	Target	Achievement	Target	Achievement
1.	Water Area Development in Hectare						
	(a) FFDA, Bank Finance in ha	16.00	15.21	16.00	23.27	20.00	28.54
	(b) Without Bank Finance (ha)	9.00	9.88	9.00	9.97	9.00	8.62
	Total	25.00	25.09	25.00	30.24	29.00	37.16
2.	SGSY (ha)		262.30		273.81		184.06
3.	Prawn Seed stocking in lakh	10.00	12.97	10.00	12.71	10.00	10.15
4.	Subsidy released in lakh	--	4.90		8.06	-	6.47

Source : Unpublished record of District Fisheries office-cum-CEO, Berhmapur.

Table 3.30 reveals the performance of FFDA during the part three years 2003-04, 2004-05, and 2005-06. In the year 2004-05 and 2005-06 achievement is more than the target which is a healthy sign.

Development of Reservoir Fisheries

The Ganjam district is endowed with a good number of open water bodies in the form of reservoirs/MIPs. These resources are untapped/underutilized due to lack of systematic policy for development of fisheries. Keeping in view of the above the State Government has formulated "State Reservoir Fishery Policy". According to this aid policy the fishing right of all the Reservoir/M.I.Ps above 40.00 hectare has been transferred to Fisheries Department. In Ganjam district so far 24 numbers of such Reservoirs/M.I.Ps with water spread area of 2883 hectare has been identified. As the above Reservoirs/M.I.Ps have been tagged to PFC Society/SHGs on long-term lease basis and fish seed have been stocked The detail of above Reservoirs/M.I.Ps is follows:

1.	Number of Reservoir/M.I.Ps above 40.00 ha	:	24
2.	Water spread area	:	2883.00 hectare
3.	Number of women SHG tagged	:	24
4.	Number of PFCS tagged	:	13
5.	Quantity of fish seed stocked	:	72.50 lakh
6.	Royalty, lease value etc. collected	:	Rs.9.80 lakh

Development of Captive Nurseries

To facilitate stocking of advanced fingerlings in the reservoirs captive nurseries for 10.61 hectare water area near 22 reservoirs.

Pisciculture through Women SHGs (Self-help Group)

During the year 2001-02 it was attempted to promote pisciculture through SHGs by giving GP tanks on long-term lease basis. The result was quite encouraging. Being encouraged with the success of pisciculture through SHGs the other SHGs came forward to involve themselves in fisheries activities. Now emphasis has been given to promote pisciculture through women SHGs by providing long-term lease of G.P tanks and MIPs. It is depicted in Table 3.31.

Table 3.31. Pisciculture Through Women Self-help Group (Up to 2004-05)

(In No)

Sl. No.	Type of water body tagged	No	Area in hectare	No. of SHGs tagged (in number)	Total Women members
1.	GP Tanks	509	668.80	421	5017
2.	MIPs	11	547.00	24	328
	Total	520	1215.80	445	5345

Source: Unpublished record of District Fisheries office cum-CEO, Berhmapur.

Table 3.31 indicates that pisciculture through women SHGs has shown encouraging result and the total women member went up to 5345. A total of 445 SHGs have been tagged towards development of pisciculture. A total of 520 water bodies are tagged.

Chapter

Role of Different Banks in Financing the Fishermen

Evolution of Banking Institution

It is important to analyse the origin of banking before going into the evolution of banking institutions. Since the banking activities were started in different periods in different countries there is no unanimity regarding the origin of the word 'Bank'. The word 'Bank' is said to have derived from the French word "Banco' or 'Bancus' or 'Banque' which means a "bench'.

The evolution of modern banking institution can be traced into three ancestors such as :

(*i*) Goldsmiths.

(*ii*) Moneylenders and

(*iii*) Merchant Bankers.

The evolution of commercial banking can be traced to the practice of safekeeping of gold and other valuables with goldsmiths/money lenders/merchants. The first banking institution was the 'Bank of Venice" established in Italy in the year 1157. The Bank of England was established in 1694 on Italian lines.

Commercial banks are the oldest banking institutions in the organized sector. They constitute the predominant segment of banking system in India. The cater to the needs of trade, commerce, industries, agriculture, small business, transport and other activities with a wide network of branches throughout the country. Commercial banks command a major share in the total banking operations.

Functions of Commercial Bank

The functions of commercial bank are broadly classified under two heads: acceptance of deposits and granting of loans.

As the name implies, commercial banks are those banks which receive deposits from the public and lend money for trading industry and commerce. They concentrate mainly on commercial and trading activities. Generally they receive deposits from the public which are repayable on demand. There are different types of deposit. They are fixed deposits, current account deposits, saving bank deposits. They also lend to traders and manufacturers for short periods. Furthur they provide working capital to business in the form of overdraft and cash credit. Furthermore, they discount bills of exchange and thereby extend finance for the promotion of trade. Besides these, they provide a number of agency services such as collection of cheques, payment of insurance premium and provide general utility services such as safe keeping of valuable commodities, issue letter of credit, remittance of funds etc. The services of commercial banks are ever expanding with the change in the needs and requirements of the society and today they have come forward to take up the role of development bankers as well.

Classification of Commercial Banks

The classification of commercial bank is illustrated below. On the basis of statutory provision:

(*i*) Scheduled Bank

(*ii*) Non-Scheduled Bank

On the Basis of ownership :

(*i*) Public Sector Bank

(*ii*) Private Sector Bank

On the Basis of Domicile :

(*i*) Indian Bank

(*ii*) Foreign Bank

Commercial banks in India may broadly be classified into the following:

(*i*) Statutory,

(*ii*) Ownership and

(*iii*) Domicile.

I. Statutory:

On the statutory basis commercial banks may be classified into two types namely: Scheduled banks and Non-scheduled Banks.

These are those commercial banks which are included in the Second Schedule of the Reserve Bank of India Act, 1934. The following conditions must be fulfilled to qualify for inclusion in the Second Schedule of the RBI Act, 1934.

(*i*) The bank must have a minimum paid-up capital and reserves of Rs. 5 lakh.

(*ii*) The bank must be either a company or a corporation whether it is incorporated in India or outside but carrying on the business of banking in India.

(*iii*) The Bank must satisfy' the Reserve Bank of India that its activities are not being conducted in a manner detrimental to the interest of the depositors.

Presently the Reserve Bank of India has prescribed a minimum capital of Rs. 100 crores for starting a new commercial Bank. The schedule banks have to abide by all the rules, regulations and directions issued by the Reserve Bank of India from time to time.

II. Ownership

On the basis of ownership, the commercial Banks may be classified into two types.

(*i*) Public sector banks and

(*ii*) Private sector banks.

I. Public Sector Banks : Public sector banks are those banks which are owned by the Government of India. The

Government of India enter into the field of banking in the year 1955 with the establishment of the state Bank of India. Public Sector banks include:

(*i*) The State Bank of India

(*ii*) Associate Banks of State Bank of India

(*iii*) Nationalised Banks

(*iv*) Regional Rural Banks.

II. Private Sector Banks : Private sector banks are those banks which are established by the private bodies. The Indian banking recognise the significance of private sector banking under the liberalisation process. The private sector banking consists of :

(*i*) Private scheduled commercial banks

(*ii*) Private foreign banks

(*iii*) Private Non-scheduled commercial Banks

(*iv*) Local Area Banks.

III. Domicile

On the basis of domicile, commercial banks may be classified into two types:

(*i*) Indian Banks and

(*ii*) Foreign Banks.

(i) Indian Banks: Indian banks are those banks which are incorporated in India under the law of Indian Government and doing the business of banking in India.

(ii) Foreign Banks: Foreign banks are those banks which are incorporated outside India under the law of that country but doing the business of banking in India. For example. The Chartered Bank, The Grindlays Banks, The Lloyds Bank etc.

Non-scheduled Banks

Banks which are not included in the second schedule of the Reserve Bank of India are called non-scheduled banks. They are not entitled to enjoy the facilities which the scheduled banks enjoy.

Nationalisation of Banks in India

The process of nationalisation of banks started with the nationalisation of the Reserve Bank of India in the year 1949. It was followed by the nationalisation of the Imperial Bank of India in the year 1955. However, the major nationalisation event took place on Saturday, July 19, 1969, when 14 Scheduled commercial banks with more than Rs. 50 crores of deposits were nationalized. The list of nationalised banks and the compensation paid to shareholders are illustrated in table 4.1.

Table 4.1. Details of Bank Nationalised in India

Name of the Bank	Compensation paid (Rs. in crores)
The Bank of India Ltd.	14.7
The United Bank of India Ltd.	4.2
The Central Bank of India Ltd.	17.5
The Union Bank of India Ltd.	3.1
The United Commercial Bank Ltd.	4.2
The Bank of Baroda Ltd.	8.4 .
The Punjab National Bank Ltd.	10.2
The Canara Bank Ltd.	3.6
The Dena Bank Ltd.	3.6
The Indian Overseas Bank Ltd.	2.5
The Syndicate Bank Ltd.	3.6
The Bank of Maharastra Ltd.	2.3
The Indian Bank Ltd.	2.3
The Allahbad Bank	3.1

Source: Commercial Banking by Gordon & Natarajan, p. 60.

Table 4.1 shows the name of the 14 commercial banks with compensation paid to them. The Bank of India leads with a maximum compensation of 14.7 crores.

Again six more major Scheduled banks with deposits of over Rs. 200 crores were nationalised on April 15, 1980. This is shown in Table 4.2.

Table 4.2. Nationalisation of Scheduled Banks in India

Name of the Bank	Compensation paid (Rs. in crore)
The Andhra Bank Ltd.	6.1
The New Bank of India Ltd.	5.1
The Punjab and Sind Bank Ltd.	1.8
The Corporation Bank Ltd.	2.1
The Oriental Bank of Commerce Ltd.	2.4
The Vijaya Bank Ltd.	1.0

Source: Commercial Banking by Gordon and Natarajan p. 60.

Table 4.2 shows that the no. of Scheduled banks nationalised in second phase along with compensation paid. The Andhra Bank Ltd. has received the maximum compensation of Rs. 6.1 crore, followed by the New Bank of India Ltd. The Vijaya Bank Ltd. has received the lowest compensation of Rs. 1 crore.

Structure of Indian Banking System

Indian banking network structure in one of the largest in the world. It includes both Scheduled banks and Non-scheduled banks which is depicted in Table 4.3.

Table 4.3 shows the structure of Indian banking systems along with other banks. It specifically deals with commercial banking system in India. Which contains both Scheduled banks and non-scheduled banks.

Scheduled Commercial Banks in Orissa

In Orissa the branches cf public sector banks are 1408 and the total private sector banks are 19. There are 834 Regional Rural Banks (RRBs) in the State. Hence the branches of all the commercial banks comes to 2261. There are also 321 co-operative banks. The performance of all scheduled commercial banks is described in Table 4.4.

Table 4.3. Structure of Indian Banking System

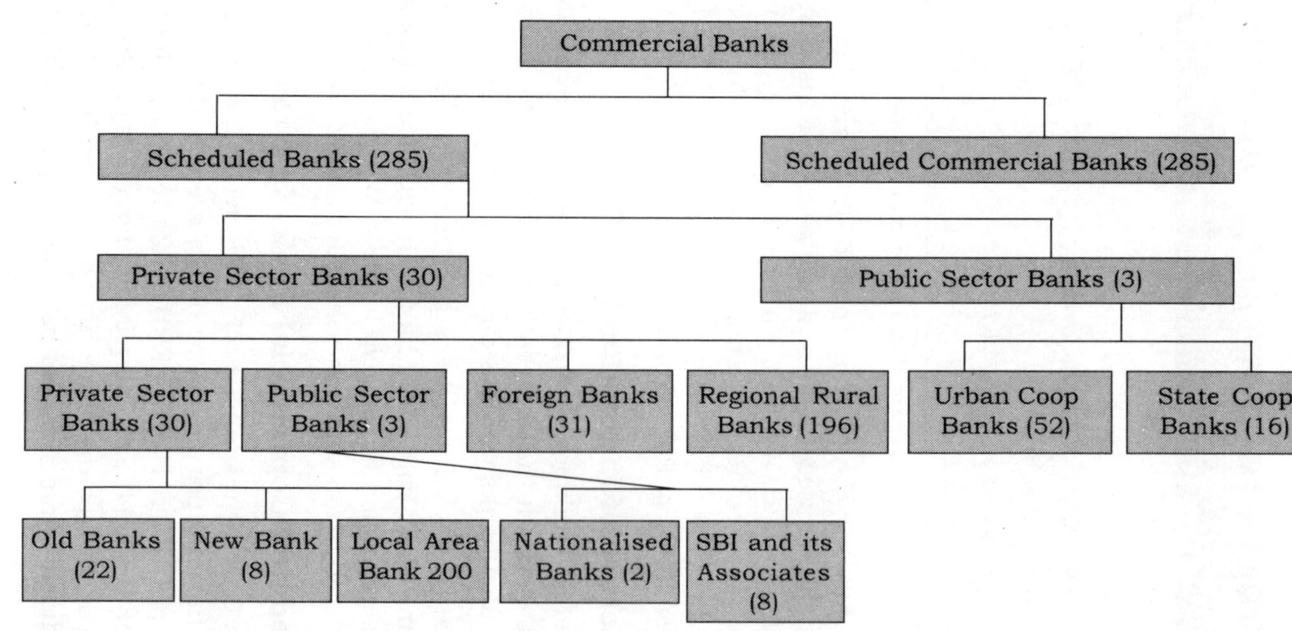

Source: Commercial Banking by Garden & Natarajan, p. 8

Table 4.4. Performance of All Scheduled Commercial Banks in Orissa

(as on 31-3-2005)

Sl. No.	Year	No. of Branches	Aggregate deposits (Rs. in Crore)	Gross bank credit (Rs. in Crore)	Credit-deposit Ratio (%)
1.	2000-01	2,214	15,110.87	6,264.98	41.46
2.	2001-02	2,224	18,689.18	8,527.15	45.63
3.	2002-03	2,232	20,347.87	10,430.71	51.26
4.	2003-04	2,242	23,359.86	13,390.53	57.32
5.	2004-05	2,261	27,372.64	17,587.83	64.25

Source: Economic Survey, Government of Orissa, Bhubaneswar, 2005-06, pp. 13/2.

Table 4.4 shows that aggregate deposit have been advanced from 15,110.87 crore in 2000-01 to 27,372 in the year 2004-05. Credit-deposit ratio has also been increased by 60 per cent from the year 2000-01.

Banking Network in Ganjam District

The district Ganjam is served by one of the largest network of bank branches. This is reflected in Table 4.5.

Table 4.5. Banking Network in Ganjam District in 2006

Sl. No.	Type of Institution	No	Branches
1.	Commercial Banks	21	124
2.	Regional Rural Banks	01	66
3.	Central coop Banks	02	31
4.	CARD Bank	01	04
5.	Orissa State Co-op. Bank	01	01
6.	Orissa State Financial Corporation	01	01
	Total	27	227

Source: Potential linked credit plan, NABARD 2007, p. 114.

Table 4.5 shows that there are 226 branches of 26 banks and one branch of OSFC operating in the district. Commercial Banks have the highest number of branches (124) followed by Regional Rural Banks with 66 branches.

Aggregate Deposit of Gross Bank Credit

Table 4.6 illustrates aggregate deposits and gross bank credit by commercial banks in Ganjam district.

Table 4.6. Aggregate Deposit and Gross Bank Credit of Scheduled Commercial Banks in Ganjam District (as on 31st March)

Sl.No.	Unit	2002	2003	2004
A. Public Sector Banks				
1. Reporting Offices	No	124	126	127
2. Deposits	Rs. in lakhs	138773	153191	163400
3. Credit	Rs. in lakhs	40,590	44,475	56500
4. Credit-deposit Ratio	Per cent	29.25	29.03	34.58
B. Regional Rural Banks				
1 . Reporting Offices	No	64	64	64
2. Deposits	Rs. In lakhs	24844	27862	30800
3. Credit	Rs. in lakhs	9475	11759	14300
4. Credit-Deposits Ratio	Per cent	38.14	42.20	46.43
C. All Scheduled Commercial Banks				
1. Reporting Offices	No	189	191	191
2. Deposit	Rs. in lakhs	166330	183824	19420
3. Credit	Rs. in lakhs	50261	56373	70700
4. Credit-Deposit Ratio	Per cent	30.22	30.67	36.41

Source : District Statistical Handbook, Ganjam 2005 P-81

Table 4.6 indicates that there is an increase in deposits by the public sector bank. The credit-deposit ratio has also increased from 29.25 per cent during the year 2002 to 34.58 per cent in the year 2004. Similarly Regional Rural Banks records a growth in deposits. The credit-deposit ratio record a growth of 38.14 per cent in 2002 to 46.43 per cent during the year 2004.

Acceptance of Deposits

The acceptance of deposits of different banks are shown in Table 4.7.

Table 4.7. Deposits by Commercial Banks, RRBs and Coop. Banks in Ganjam as on 31-03-2006

(Rs. in lakhs)

Sl. No.	Agency	No. of Branches	Deposits 2003-04	Deposits 2004-05	Deposits 2005-06	% of share as on 31.3.06
1.	Commercial Banks	124	1,48,533 (3%)	16,1,060 (8%)	1,84,888 (15%)	78
2.	Regional Rural Bank (RRBs)	66	30,736 (10%)	31,542 (3%)	33,232 (5%)	14
3.	Co-operative Banks Banks	32	25,349 (37%)	26,056 (3%)	19,630 (25%)	8
	Total	222	20,4,618.00 (7%)	218658 (7%)	237750 (9%)	100

Source: Potential linked credit plan, NABARD, Ganjam 2007-08, p. 11.

Table 4.7 shows that the growth rate of mobilisation of deposits by commercial banks and RRBs has increased by 15 per cent and 5 per cent respectively during 2005-06. However deposit of Co-operative Banks have decreased by 25 per cent during 2005-06 compared to the position obtained during the previous year 2004-05. Commercial banks continue to have largest share of deposits, constituting about 78 per cent of total deposits.

Loan Outstanding

The agency-wise credit outstanding is expressed in Table 4.8.

Table 4.8 shows that commercial banks still plays a major role in the credit portfolio of the district as compared it previous year, despite a decline of six per cent points commercial banks tops the list with loan outstanding amount to 67 per cent followed by RRBs with 16 per cent and co-operative bank with 17 per cent.

Table 4.8. Outstanding Loans by Commercial Banks, RRBs and Coop. Banks of Ganjam as on 1-3-2006

(Rs. in lakhs)

Sl. No.	Agency	No. of Branches	Loan outstanding 2003-04	2004-05	2005-06	% of share
1.	Commercial Banks	124	51,149.00	94,373.00	88,293.00	67%
2.	RRBs	66	14,266.00	17,505.00	20,856.00	16%
3.	Co-op Banks	32	18501.00	19,804.00	22,199.00	17%
	Total	222	8916.00	131718.00	131348.00	100%

Source: Potential linked credit plan, NABARD, p. 117.

Role of Commercial Banks in Ganjam District

All commercial banks participate in the implementation of the Government programmes and schemes. The apex level financial institution namely National Bank for Agriculture and Rural Development (NABARD), National Co-operative Development Corporation (NCDC), Fish Farmers Development Agency (FFDA), refinance commercial banks who in turn finance the individual fishermen, Self-help Group (SHG) etc.

At the State level, the credit requirement of the fishermen is estimated by the State Level Bankers Committee (SLBC), to provide credit to the fisheries sector as a vehicle combining both marine and inland fisheries. The NABARD's refinance assistance of inland and marine fishery sector also play's an important role.

The State and Central Governments make joint efforts to improve the common infrastructure facilities. The facilities are as fallows-landing sites marketing support, godown, ice plant, and cold storage facilities, provision for diesel supply for mechanized boats at a subsidised prices.

Only two schemes are meant for upliftment of fishermen living below the poverty line and are routed through commercial banks. The beneficiaries are jointly selected by Department of Fisheries and Panchayat Raj (DFPR) at the Block level for getting subsidies from the DRDA.

Fish Farmers Development Agency (FFDA)

Again commercial banks play an important role in successfull implementation of the programme. FFDA, which is a Centrally sponsored scheme established during the year 1976.

Brackish Water Development Agencies (BFDA)

To improve the economic conditions of fishermen of Chilika lake, Rusululya and Bahuda estuarine system on five coastal blocks and a land-based scheme is launched by Brackish Water Development Agencies established as a Centrally Sponsored scheme, started in the year 1989-90. The Agency identifies feasible area and recommends for shrimp fanning and prepares project report, to be sponsored by commercial banks.

The credit facilities from bank caters to the need of only 19 per cent, who are selected under the various fishermen development programmes. To sum up bank only provides the subsidy loan to the fishermen routed through the Department of Fisheries, Government of Orissa. Rate of interest is charged as per Reserve Bank of India rules and the duration period between 1 to 3 years.

Re-Finance to Bank by FFDA

The FFDA has re-financed the commercial banks to finance in inland fisheries. The amount of refinance to different Commercial banks is shown in Table 4.9.

Table 4.9 shows financial assistance made to different banks by FFDA sector from the year 2003-04 to 2005-06. Banks finance has increased from 28,979 lakhs during 2003-04 to 99.26 lakhs during the year 2005-06. RRBs are playing an important role in contributing 25.05 per cent of

Table 4.9. Finances made to the FFDA by the Different Banks of the District

(Area in Hectare/Amount in Lakh)

Sl. No.	Name of the Bank	Year 2003-04			Year 2004-05			Year 2005-06		
		No	Area	Amount	No	Area	Amount	No	Area	Amount
1.	RRB	10	4.32	7.250	20	14.07	24.650	36	16.60	45.790
2.	Andhra Bank	01	0.26	0.690	07	2.38	3.490	12	6.60	16.240
3.	State Bank of India	04	0.92	2.110	10	9.88	17.900	18	12.20	25.670
4.	CARD	24	12.68	7.708	01	0.12	0.840	01	0.38	2.720
5.	Bank of India	01	1.34	3.030	04	2.70	3.100	01	1.84	3.400
6.	Bank of Baroda	01	0.30	0.630	01	0.12	0.360	—	—	—
7.	United Bank of India	01	0.62	0.624	01	0.64	0.500	—	—	—
8.	Central Bank of India	—	—	—	01	0.28	0.280	—	—	—
9.	Canara Bank	—	—	1.487	—	—	—	—	—	—
10.	Indian Bank	02	0.58	1.880	0.3	1.3	2.080	02	0.40	0.480
11.	Indian Overseas Bank	03	1.28	3.570	02	0.82	1.300	04	206	4.060
12.	Union Bank of India	—	—	—	—	—	—	01	0.30	0.500
13.	Uco Bank	—	—	—	—	—	01	0.35	0.400	
	Total	47	22.30	28.979	50	32.59	54.500	76	40.73	96.260

Source: District Fisheries Office-cum-CEO (BFDA/FFDA), Ganjam, Berhampur.

Table 4.10. Block-wise Finance by Different Banks under FFDA in Ganjam District

(Area in Hectare/Amount in Lakh)

Sl. No.	Name of the Block	Year 2003-04			Year 2004-05			Year 2005-06		
		No.	Area	Amount	No. of Banks	Area	Amount	No. of Banks	Area	Amount
1	2	3	4	5	6	7	8	9	10	11
1.	Ganjam	1	0.26	0.540	2	0.96	0.750	5	3.08	7.61
2.	Polasara	1	0.40	0.135	2	0.28	0.350	5	4.20	4.51
3.	Beguniapara	1	0.30	0.750	5	3.16	3.800	2	1.96	3.37
4.	Purusottampur	8	2.38	1.550	4	5.22	6.900	8	3.52	9.73
5.	K.S. Nagar	—	—	0.400	2	0.57	0.350	1	0.56	2.15
6.	Chatrapur	—	—	—	—	—	—	—	—	—
7.	Hinjilicut	1	0.28	0.560	—	—	—	3	1.02	4.19
8.	Khallikote	4	1.40	2.855	4	0.78	1.980	6	1.20	2.33
9.	Rangeilunda	—	—	0.300	2	2.90	8.140	1	0.96	4.00
10.	Kukudakhandi	1	0.30	0.630	1	0.12	0.350	3	0.93	1.05
11.	Sanakhemundi	—	—	—	—	—	—	7	6.56	14.69
12.	Digapahandi	—	—	—	—	—	—	6	1.70	3.68
13.	Chikiti	2	0.65	0.840	—	—	—	3	1.56	4.30

1	2	3	4	5	6	7	8	9	10	11
14.	Patrapur	—	—	—	2	0.24	0.200	1	0.26	0.45
15.	Bhanjanagar	9	5.19	6.672	8	4.20	8.300	11	5.06	16.31
16.	Bellaguntha	2	2.54	6.026	3	5.40	5.850	1	0.16	2.00
17.	Jaganathprasad	6	2.92	1.691	3	0.64	1.200	2	1.98	4.30
18.	Buguda	—	—	0.260	4	1.76	1.900	3	0.72	2.50
19.	Dharakote	2	1.06	1.656	—	—	0.300	—	—	—
20.	Aska	4	1.86	3.264	4	1.52	2.200	3	1.22	2.70
21.	Shengada	—	—	—	2	0.72	0.580	2	9.26	1.02
22.	Sorada	5	2.76	0.850	3	4.12	11.350	3	3.52	8.30
	Total	47	22.30	28.979	50	32.59	54.500	76	40.73	99.26

Source: District Fisheries Office-cum-CEO (BFDA/FFDA), Ganjam, Berhampur.

total finance during the year 2003-04, 45 per cent of total finance during the year 2004-05 and 46.13 per cent in the year 2005-06. The total area covered has also been increased from 22.30 hectare in 2003-04 to 40.73 hectare during the year 2005-06.

Block-wise finance by different banks in FFDA sector is shown in Table 4.10.

Table 4.10 indicates that out of 22 Blocks of the district in the year 2003-04 and 2004-05, Bhanjanagar receiving the highest amount and Chatrapur Block have not received any finance in FFDA sector.

Progress of Pond Development

Commercial banks have financed for the development and renovation of ponds under Swa Rozagar Yojana Scheme. The quantum of finance being made to different blocks of the district under this scheme is shown in Table 4.11.

Table 4.11 shows progress of pond development in FFDA sector. It marked an increase of Rs. 273.811akhs during the year, 2004-05 but there is a fall during the year 2005-06 to Rs. 117.3 lakh. Number of ponds.have also decreased from 124 to 93.

Co-operatives

Co-operatives play a very important role in economic development of fishermen in the district. The basic idea behind the co-operative movement is to promote savings, self-help and mutual help through, democratic management. The fishery co-operative societies were reorganized in 1959 as per recommendations of A.F. Laid, a Canadian Expert in Fishery Co-operatives. The fishery co-operatives were brought under the control of Fisheries Directorate from October 1973 for better organization and proper management of financial resources.

The basic objectives of fishery co-operatives, in the early stage is to provide credit to fishermen. It did not fulfil the main aim of making the fishermen self-reliant and free from the clutches of money-lenders and middlemen. The loans taken from the co-operatives were not repaid in right time, making the co-operatives defaulters due to heavy overdue.

Table 4.11. Progress of Pond Development under S.G.S.Y.

(Area in Hectare/Amount in Lakh)

Sl. No.	Name of the Bank	Year 2003-04			Year 2004-05			Year 2005-06		
		No. of ponds	Area	Amount	No. of ponds	Area	Amount	No. of ponds	Area	Amount
1	2	3	4	5	6	7	8	9	10	11
1.	Ganjam	4	282	0.500	3	4	2.30	7	5.60	16.950
2.	Polsara	7	19.2	3.600	8	13	24.40	5	11.60	11.75
3.	Beguniapada	4	17.86	6.000	5	5	5.40	4	6.39	5.120
4.	Purushottampur	11	30.80	7.000	11	23	24.40	7	23.00	7.550
5.	Kabisuryanagar	2	8	2.200	4	4	10.81	3	2.96	7.600
6.	Chatrapur	5	4.8	2.800	13	13	28.00	9	13.15	9.050
7.	Hinjilicut	4	14	2.400	8	9	23.00	3	10.80	2.800
8.	Khallikote	2	5.84	2.120	4	5	14.78	2	5.40	5.600
9.	Rangeilunda	1	1.6	2.200	10	15	5.40	8	15.80	13.900
10.	Kukudakhandi	2	4.8	3.100	4	4	11.00	3	8.00	7.150
11.	Sanakhemundi	10	57.40	14.660	7	10	4.60	13	23.20	31.960
12.	Digapahandi	7	5.6	4.120	5	6	54.76	1	40.00	2.560
13.	Chikiti	—	—	—	—	—	—	—	—	—

1	2	3	4	5	6	7	8	9	10	11
14.	Patapur	4	13	8.000	7	7	26.60	4	10.20	9.400
15.	Bhanjanagar	2	1.4	1.380	3	4	2.15	3	1.80	6.540
16.	Bellaguntha	5	7.15	8.985	8	12	13.96	6	6.10	8.850
17.	Jagannath Prasad	4	42.2	7.670	4	4	3.34	6	7.28	16.400
18.	Buguda	3	12	2.390	4	6	4.43	1	3.00	1.260
19.	Dharakote	1	0.63	2.000	1	1	0.30	1	2.50	1.000
20.	Aska	3	3.9	3.198	5	5	3.88	4	4.00	4.20
21.	Sheragada	2	2.8	0.800	5	5	5.00	—	—	—
22.	Sorada	4	7.2	2.400	5	5	5.00	3	3.20	3.500
	Total	87	263.00	87.523	124	160	273.81	93	20398	117.360

Source: District Fisheries Office-cum-CEO (BFDA/FFDA), Berhampur.

The objectives of fishery co-operative are as follows:

1. To help the members marketing their catch.
2. To provide subsidised purchase of fishing crafts.
3. To procure loans from institutional sources for the socio economic development of the members of the society.
4. To help the members to adopt modern method of technology in fishing.
5. To provide the idea of mutual help and Co-ordination among the members for common interest for the development of the society.

Fisheries Co-operatives

The National Co-operative Development Corporation (NCDC) and commercial banks provide loan to the beneficiaries through the PMFCS. About eight per cent of the total Government loans were provided to the marine sector. The NCDC and NABARD Finance term loans and working capital to PMFCSs and to Apex societies which in turn finances to primary societies. Under the Societies Act. 1960, three societies were registered in 1996 which included Sonepur, Patisonapur and Gopalpur. Many of the societies are defaulters due to non-repayment of loan to Government Apex Co-operatives and commercial banks. The PMFCSs in the district are not taking any steps towards marketing of fish caught by the members of the societies finance made to co-operative are shown in Table 4.12.

Table 4.12 shows that 32 BLCs have been provided to fisheris (maxine) loan through different PFCS. The total loan amount availed by these PFCSs amounted to Rs. 13,48,292 lakhs, but none of these societies have repaid the loan as on 31-03-2006 and the total loan amount has increased to Rs. 23,81,029 lakhs.

Co-Operatives in Mechanized Fishing

The mechanized fishing were taken up by the Co-operatives in the district is mainly through MPFCS which

Table 4.12. NCD. : Loan Position as on 31-03-2006

(Rs. in lakh)

District	No. of BLC availed	Name of the PFCS	Amount of loan availed	Principal interest	Balance outstanding	Total (5+6) (in lakhs)
1	2	3	4	5	6	7
Ganjam	6	Gopalpur PMFCS	2,46,792	60,683	1,15,941	1,76,624
Ganjam	3	New Boxipati	2,14,750	1,22,917	1,54,933	2,77,850
Ganjam	5	Badaryapalli	2,36,250	1,45,057	1,83,562	3,28,619
Ganjam	3	Patisasanpur	1,41,750	95,097	1,64,464	2,59,561
Ganjam	5	Sana Aryapalli	2,36,250	5,85,54	1,04,963	1,63,517
Ganjam	5	Sana Nolia Nua Gaon	2,36,250	2,36,250	3,51,179	5,87,429
Ganjam	5	Bada Nolia Nua Gaon	2,36,250	2,36,250	3,51,179	5,87,429
Total	32		13,48,292	9,54808	14,26,221	23,81,029

Source: Records from Assistant Director of fisheries (marine). Ganjam.

Table 4.13. Development of Marine Fisheries Through Motorization of Traditional crafts up to 31-03-2004

(Amount in lakh)

Sl. No.	Name of the Bank	2003-04		2004-05		2005-06	
		No. of Boats	Amount	No. of Boats	Amount	No. of Boats	Amount
1.	RGB, Chatrapur	09	3,78,000	05	2,20,000	04	1,68,000
2.	Allahabad Bank, Gopalpur Port	08	3,36,000	—	—	04	1,68,000
3.	S.B.I., Chatrapur	05	2,20,000	02	84,000	10	4,20,000
4.	S.B.I., Ganjam	01	42,000	—	—	—	—
5.	RGB,Korapalli	07	2,94,000	06	2,52,000	11	4,62,000
6.	RGB, Sonepur	04	1,68,000	02	84,000	02	84,000
7.	Andhra Bank, Gopalpur	08	3,36,000	01	42.000	01	42,000
8.	Andhra Bank, Gopalpur	02	84,000	—	—	—	—
9.	RGB, Huma	—	—	02	84,000	08	3,36,000
10.	Allahabad Bank, Aryapalli	—	—	—	—	04	1,68,000
11.	Andhra Bank, Gopalpur Port	—	—	—	—	02	84,000
	Total	44	18,58,000	18	7,66,000	46	19,32,000

Source: Collected from the records of ADF, Marine - Ganjam.

are functioning in the district. It has been found that most of the societies and number of the BLCs are default due to heavy overdues and some of the MFCs were also liquidated during 1996-97 in Ganjam district. This is shown in Table 4.13.

Table 4.13 shows motorisation of traditional crafts in marine sector. During the year 2003-04 the number of total motorised boats are 44, with a finance of Rs. 18,58,000 by banks. It has decreased to 18 during the year 2004-05 but again number of motorisation of boats have increased to 46 with a bank finance of Rs. 19,32,000.

Reservoir Policy

This policy comes under co-operative sector. The policy was started by the Government in inland sector known as State Reservoir policy. Information of about this policy is depicted in Table 4.14.

Table 4.14 shows that a total amount of Rs. 1,0,00,620 is spent towards renovation of 24 reservoirs, MIP's under State Reservoir Policy.

For the socio-economic development of fishermen both inland and marine sectors there are 36 number of PFCSs functioning in the district. There are 15 marine PFCSs having 3495 members and 21 Inland PFCSs having 3039 members. Out of 15 marine PFCSs, 6 PFCSs are exclusively women PFCSs which are included in STEP programme.

National Bank for Agricultural and Rural Development (NABARD)

The Reserve Bank of India since its inception has extended short-term and long-term credit through state Co-operative banks and land development banks. The RBI felt the need for an agency at the national level that to provide all types of credit to various sectors in rural economy such as agriculture, small scale industries, small and cottage industries, artisans, handicrafts etc. in an integrated way for rural development. The committee for review arrangements for institutional credit for agricultural and rural development was set up by the Reserve Bank of India in 1979. It has recommended in its report for setting up of NABARD. Hence, the Government of India passed National Bank for Agricultural Rural

Development Bill in Parliament in Dec. 1981 and the NABARD came into existence in July, 1952. NABARD has taken the entire refinancing function of R.B.I. NABARD plays an important role towards fishery development in Orissa. For more information detail see Table 4.15

Table 4.14. Information as on Reservoirs/MIP's under state Reservoir Policy during 2005-06

Sl. No.	Name of the Reservoir MIP	20% of lease amount towards Govt. revenue (in Rs.)	80% of lease amount towards seed cost (in Rs.)	Royality of WR Dept. (in Rs.)	Total (in Rs.) (3+4+5)	No. of finger-lings stocked
1	2	3	4	5	6	7
1.	Salia	10800	43200	7200	61200	4.32
2.	Marood	4200	16800	2800	23800	3.60
3.	Jhamai MIP	2520	10080	1680	14280	1.36
4.	Dhanei	6000	24000	4000	34000	3.00
5.	Bada Haja MIP	4320	17280	2880	24480	1.72
6.	Damiamaru Ghai	2520	10080	1680	14280	1.00
7.	Humar ampara	16500	66000	11000	93500	7.21
8.	Raghunath Sagar	3600	14400	2400	20400	1.50
9.	Gopal Ganda MIP	3000	12000	2000	17000	3.00
10.	Khajra Banka MIP	2520	10080	1680	14280	1.50
11.	Bhalu Ghai	2520	10080	1680	14280	1.50
12.	Lankagada MIP	2460	9840	1640	13940	1.01
13.	Chamunda Ghai	3000	12000	2000	17000	1.21
14.	Ghodahad	9000	36000	60000	51000	4.24
15.	Kayna Nala MP	3000	12000	2000	17000	1.00
16.	Kanhei Nala MIP	3600	14400	2400	20400	1.20
17.	Ganla Nalo MIP	3000	12000	2000	17000	1.00
18.	Baghalati	12000	48000	8000	68000	4.89
19.	Bhanjanagar	15000	60000	10000	85000	6.66
20.	Daha	16500	66000	11000	93500	6.60
21.	Debi Jhar MIP	3000	12000	2000	17000	1.50
22.	Baghua	21000	84000	14000	119000	8.26
23.	Soroda	24000	96000	16000	136000	9.70
24.	Alikuan MIP	2520	10080	1680	14280	1.00
	Total	178580	706320	117720	1000620	77.50

Source : Collected from the records of Assistant Director of Fsheries, cum CEO, (BFDA/FFDA) Berhampur.

Table 4.15. Refinance Assistance to Fisheries Sector Provided by NABARD in Orissa during the year 2004-05

(Rs in lakh)

Sl. No.	Purpose	CBS	SCB	SLDB	RRBS	Total
1.	Inland fishing	11.051	19.389	89.079	37.789	157.308
2.	Marine fishing	1.269	—	—	0.378	1.647
3.	Brackish fishing	19.581	9.277	—	0.689	29.547

Source: Economic Survey, Government of Orissa, Bhubaneswar, 2005-06, p. 13/12.

Table 4.15 shows refinance to fishery sector during the year 2004-05 and 2005-06., where inland fishery have receive a lion's share of Rs. 157.308 lakh.

Contribution of NABARD in Fishery Sector of Ganjam District

The NABARD plays an important role in developing fishery sector of Ganjam District Table 4.16 shows the credit flow by NABARD relating to different fishery activities of the district. Tank fishereies has a major share in comparison

Table 4.16. Contribution of NABARD in Fishery Sector of Ganjam District

(Rs in lakh)

Sl. No.	Activity	2003-04	2004-05	2005-06
1.	Tank fisheries	78.26	147.76	117.07
2.	Reservoir unit	9.56	33.64	38.68
3.	Fish hatcheries	0.13	19.88	4.08
4.	Motorized boats	6.63	12.22	22.69
5.	Non-motorized boats	22.65	27.88	2.00
6.	Miscellaneous	29.71	40.69	36.78
	Total	146.94	282.07	221.30

Source: Potential linked credit plan 2007-08, NABARD, Ganjam p. 59.

to other activities. It has increased to 117.07 lakh during the year 2005.06 from 78.26 lakh during the year 2003-04. It shows a decrease trend in the year 2005-06 Rs. 60.77 lakhs from the year 2004-05.

Credit flow by Different Financial Institutions

Different financial institutions such as commercial banks, RRBs and Co-operative banks have provide credit for the fishery sector of Ganjam district. Table 4.17 shows an increasing trend over the past three years. In the year 2003-04 the total finance was 147 lakhs which is increased to 282 lakh in 2004-05. But in the year 2005-06 amount marked an increased with Rs. 221 lakhs. Commercial banks play an active role for development of fishery.

Table 4.17. Ground Level Credit Flow by Different Financial Institution in Ganjam District

(Rs. in lakh)

Sl. No.	Type of credit institution	2003-04		2004-05		2005-06	
		Amount disbursed	%	Amount disbursed	%	Amount disbursed	%
1.	Commercial Banks	86	59	166	59	110	50
2.	RRB	57	39	94	33	93	42
3.	Co-operative Banks	4	2	22	8	18	8
	Total	147	100	282	100	221	100

Source: Potential linked credit plan 2007-08 NABARD, Ganjam P-59.

Rushikulya Gramya Bank

The co-operative sector could not meet the vast and varied needs of rural credit, especially for the weaker section of rural population. In order to bridge the vital gap the Regional Rural Banks were set up. RRB's conceived with a plus points of both Co-operatives and commercial Banks. The major objective of the Regional Rural Banks is to develop the rural economy by providing credit and other facilities for the weaker sections of the rural community such as small farmers, marginal farmers, agricultural labourers, rural artisans and villages and cottage industrial units.

In the first instance, five RRBs were. set up on 2 October 2, 1975. The Regional Rural Banks Act, 1976 lays down various provisions for capital structure, management, Board of Directors, operational area and many other provisions. In the State of Orissa, four Regional Rural Banks were established in the year 1976, followed by three more in 1980 and two in the year 1981.

The Rushikulya Gramya Bank is the Scheduled commercial bank in the Ganjam district, is sponsored by the lead bank of Ganjam, Andhra Bank. It was incorporated in the year 1981. In terms of money this RGB has made significant contribution towards mobilisation of deposits. The RGB could mobilise deposits from rural public to the tune of Rs. 39.55 lakhs in the year of its incorporation (1981) itself.

Share Capital

The authorised share capital of the RGB is Rs.500 lakh and the paid up capital is Rs. 100 lakhs duly contributed by the share holders. Table 4.18 shows that 50 per cent of the share capital is provided by Government of India and 35 per cent share capital is provided by the lead bank of the district Andhra Bank.

Table 4.18 Share Capital of RGB in Ganjam district

Share holders	Issued and paid up capital	% of share
1. Government of India	Rs.50 Lakhs	50
2. Andhra Bank	Rs.35 Lakhs	35
3. Government of Orissa	Rs.15 Lakhs	15

Source: Potential linked Credit Plan, NABARD, 2007, P-1 14

At present RGB has 66 branches and it also keep a close liaison with Block and District level officers and actively participating in different government-sponsored schemes. Basically it provides loan for the following five categories:

(*i*) Crop loan finance,

(*ii*) Agricultural term loan finance,

(*iii*) Advances to rural artisians, self-employed and professionals,

(*iv*) Loan to small business and retail trade and

(*v*) Miscellaneous categories.

Co-operative Agriculture and Rural Development Banks (CARD)

There are four CARD Banks to cater the needs of the district under co-operative fold. They are situated at Berhampur, Chatrapur, Aska and Bhanjanagar. Their financial position is being badly affected from past five years. They are being provided with mearge financial assistance from higher financing agency.

Berhampur CCB

It is oldest Co-operative Bank functioning only in undivided Ganjam district from Dec. 1936. The bank has been catering to the credit needs of the people through 16 Branches.

Performance of PAC's

The number of profit making PACs are shown in Table 4.19 indicates that the number of profit making PACs come down to 53 during 2003-04 from 230 in 2002-03. However,

Table 4.19. Performance of PACs

Year	Total of PACs	No of PACs
2002-03	260	230
2003-04	260	53
2004-05	258	84

Source: NABARD Report 2007, p. 116.

it is indicated that out of 84 profit making societies during 2004-05, 21 societies have given dividend varying from 3 per cent to 9 per cent.

Aska Co-operative Central Bank

Aska Co-operative Central Bank is the oldest co-operative Bank of the district covering 14 blocks. It has been catering to the needs of the people through its 15 branches. 282 Co-operative societies including 192 PAC are affiliated to it. Table 4.20 shows the profit making PACs have come down from 82 in 2002-03 to 18 during 2003-04 and 22 during 2004-05 on account of in adequate provision towards bad debts, overdue interest, enhanced salary payments etc.

Table 4.20. Performance of PACS in Ganjam District

Year	Total no. of PACs	No. of PACs earning profit
2002-03	194	82
2003-04	191	18
2004-05	192	22

Source: NABARD Report 2007, P-1 16.

Development Schemes

The State Government and Central Government make joint efforts to improve the common infrastructure facilities. The facilities include landing cites marketing support, godown, ice plant and cold storage facilities and provision for diesel supply for mechnised boats at a subsidised price. But they are not provided finance through commercial banks. Only two schemes are meant for upliftment of fishermen living below the poverty line are routed through the commercial banks and co-operative banks. The beneficiaries are jointly selected by Department of Fisheries and Panchayat Raj (DFPR) at the block level for getting subsidies from the District Rural development Agency (DRDA).

Several development schemes are operating in marine sector in Ganjam district for the upliftment of the socio-economic status of fishermen of the district.

IRDP Schemes (Industrial Relation and Development Programme)

The IRDP is a joint sponsored scheme by the Central and the State governments. Each government contributing 50 per cent of the total cost. Under the IRDP the beneficiaries are identified from below poverty line (BPL) category. The beneficiaries are selected in the village from the BPL list prepared by the Block and DRDA under the guidance of DFPR extension officers along with the Sarapanch and the Ward Member of the Gram Panchayat. The four coastal blocks namely Ganjam, Chatrrapur, Rangailunda and Chikiti sponsor the list of selected beneficiaries to different banks to release loans which is subsidised by the DRDA, Ganjam at Chatrapur. The amount of subsidy depends upon the caste and category of beneficiariesy. In case of scheduled tribes the subsidy amount is 50 per cent for both marginal and small farmers. In case of backward and scheduled caste, the subsidy amount is 35 per cent for the beneficiaries belonging to marginal farmers and 35 per cent for the small farmers. The IRDP mainly covers the credit needs of the marine fishermen to purchase fishing gears and nets etc.

Bay of Bengal Programme

The Bay of Bengal Programme was started in the year 1983-84 with an objective to assist the marine fishermen in creating assets to increase their income. The emphasis was given to provide nets with a unit cost of Rs. 3,000 per individual, without any subsidy at the normal rate of interest. This was a need-based scheme started with the assistance of Swedish International Development Agency (SIDA) to provide finance to poor marine fishermen to acquire improved fishing gears for higher catch offish. This programme was discontinued since 1994-95.

Economic Rehabilitation of Rural Poor (ERRP)

The ERRP scheme was started in the year 1981-82. The objective of the scheme is to provide sustained annual income to the poorest of the poor to help them cross the poverty line. The scheme was jointly sponsored by the Central and the State Government with 80 and 20 per cent basis respectively. It was a fully subsidised scheme, with an unit cost of Rs. 2600 for each beneficiary. Assistance is provided in groups of five to eight persons mainly to purchase boat and net. From 1984-85 onwards subsidy amount was decreased from 100 per cent to 50 per cent and 50 per cent as loan. The selection and disbursement of loan is same as the IRDP. The scheme of the loan is same as the IRDP.

Accidental Insurance Scheme

It is a Centrally, sponsored scheme to cover the active marine fishermen and fisherwomen of the age group between 18 to 65 years. It was started in the year 1983-84. This scheme is now known as *Janashree Bima Yojana*. The aim is to provide financial assistance of Rs. 25,000 in case of death and Rs. 12,500 in case of disability during fishing in sea due to accidents. A premium of Rs. 12 per beneficiary for insurance covered is shared by the State and the Central governments on 50 : 50 basis. The National Federation of Fishermen's Co-operative Ltd., New Delhi is administering the scheme. The total number of fishermen/women covered during the year 2003-04 is 13,808. During 2004-05 it is 13,830 and during 2005-06 it is also 13,830. Total number of persons benefited during the year 2003-04 is one and in 2004-05 it is two.

Saving-cum-Relief Scheme

This scheme was started with an aim to assist fishermen with a cash amount to meet their consumption needs during lean season. Under this scheme, each fisherman is to contribute Rs. 20 per month for nine months during fishing season, amounting to Rs. 180. The amount with an equivalent matching grant was contributed by the

Department of Fisheries in three equal instalments of Rs. 120 per month during the lean season from April to June. The scheme has been discontinued in the State sector from 1994.

Under the Central sector each fisherman has to contribute Rs. 45 per month for 8 months amounting to Rs. 360. An equal amount is contributed by the Central and State governments which comes to a total of Rs. 1080. This is distributed to the fishermen at the rate of Rs. 27 per month in four instalments. This scheme continued till 1995-96. Under Central sector the scheme is applicable only to fishermen and women, who are the member of the Primary Marine Fisheries Co-operative Societies (PMFCs) and they are eligible to avail the scheme. Under this scheme during 2004-05, 2250 families were covered and during 2005-06, 1900 families were covered.

Mechanisation Programme/Motorisation

A Centrally-sponsored scheme for motorisation of country crafts was started in the year 1986-87. The scheme is meant for the mechanization of traditional boats with the installation of in Board Engine (IBE) and Out Board Engine (OBM). Fifty per cent is given as subsidy. The amount is Rs. 24,000 for IBE. From the year 1994-95 the loan amount has been raised to Rs. 45,000. The fifty per cent of subsidy are equally shared by the State and the Central Govrnments to the maximum of Rs. 12,000 for IBE and Rs. 10,000 for OBM. This has been raised to Rs. 26,000. The loan is provided through commercial banks. In the year 2004-05 Regional Rural Bank has sponsored 16 cases. Andhra Bank one case and State Bank of India two cases.

Beach Landing Crafts

The introduction of improved beach landing crafts for small scale fishermen under NCDC assistance was started in the year 1984-85. The basic objective of the scheme is to increase fish production through mechanization of boats, which can be operated by the traditional fishermen. The credit was routed through co-operative societies under the

Department of Fisheries. The beneficiaries were selected from the co-operative members to purchase a Beach Landing Craft (BLC). The NCDC provides assistance to Primary Marine Fishermen Co-operative Societies (PMFCSs).

The Government of India provides 50 per cent subsidies, the NCDC provided 45 per cent and the rest 5 per cent was contributed by the society or beneficiaries as margin money of the total unit cost. During the year 2004-05, 32 BLC's were availed by co-operative societies with a loan of 14,75,292.

FRP Catamarans

Introduction of FRP Catamarans is the State sector scheme started in the year 1992-93, with an objective of mechanization of traditional crafts. The unit cost of the scheme is Rs. 80,000 for purchase of hull engine and gears. The finance was estimated by the State Government. as 10 per cent of the unit cost as subsidy to the maximum of Rs. 8,000 and the rest, was given as loan by commercial banks.

Fish Marketing Container

The Directorate of Fisheries started a new scheme during 1994-95 to provide storing and marketing of fish container free of cost to the retailer fisherwomen. The basic objective is to maintain good quality of fish at the marketing places and for easy transportation. The cost of container is Rs. 500. A total number of 80 containers is issued to the district in the year 2004-05.

Fish Drying Racks

The scheme envisages to give financial support to marine fishermen belonging to fishermen co-operative society or individual fisherwoman for construction of drying racks through Oversea Development Agency (ODA). The purpose is to prepare of good quality of dry fish in hygienic condition in each landing centre. The cost of each drying rack is around Rs. 1,000, which is made up of local material.

In the year 2004-05 a total number of 70 racks is supplied to marine fishermen in Ganjam district.

National Welfare Fund

National Welfare Fund for fishermen a the Centrally-sponsored scheme started during the year 1987-88 to provide 100 low cost houses, one community hall with two toilets and five tube-wells to each fishermen village. The project cost per village is Rs. 82 lakhs. The finance is shared by both the Government of India and state Government on 50 : 50 basis. Not a single marine fisherman family is benefited under the scheme till the year 1995-96. The cost of construction per house is fixed at Rs. 25,000. This scheme is in operation in the State with the assistance of Government of India. Under this scheme in the year 2004-05, 131 low cost houses in inland sector and 82 houses in marine sector have been provided through the Self-help Group (SHG). The amount utilized for the purpose is Rs. 30.18 lakhs. Basically it provides a dwelling house to the forest BPL category of fishermen.

SGYS (Swarozagar Yojana)

Under this scheme finance is allotted to Self-help Group of at least 10 persons. Bank finances the amount through the society. Where loan is allotted to the minimum extent of Rs. 20,000. The subsidized amount is Rs. 1.25 lakh. The minimum loan amount is Rs. 2.50 lakh. In the year 2005-06 the loan amount is raised to Rs. 5 lakh. The loanee must belong to BPL category.

Kissan Credit Card

The scheme was started in the year 2005-06. Under the scheme Rs. 50,000 is sanctioned towards the purchase of boat and net. There is no subsidy provision in this scheme. But the rate of interest is as low as 7 per cent per annum.

STEP (Support to Training and Employment Programme)

The marine fishing fleet of the Ganjam district is mostly catamaran. It has been observed that a good quantity of fish is caught and sold at a negligible price due to its low market value. A portion of the above fish is converted to dry fish. In the present scenario the dry fish is prepared in crude traditional method under unhygienic conditions. Among the fishermen community the fisherwomen play an active role in the preparation of dry fish but they are mostly unorganized.

Keeping in view of the above the Government of Orissa in Fishery Department has planned to organise these women into co-operative societies and launched a scheme under STEP with an aim to provide basic training of hygienic preparation of dry fish, fish pickle and other value added products. Accordingly, so far 5 numbers of primary Fisherwomen Co-operative Societies have been organized covering 454 members. They have been trained by personnel from Integrated Fishery Project, Visakhapatnam, a Government of India origanisation. To facilitate the programme infrastructural support like dry fish godown, fish drying platform, tube-wells etc. are envisaged in the scheme. During the time of study it has been proposed to organize 6 number of women Primary Fishing Cooperative Societies (PFCSs) covering 546 fisherwomen under the project.

Chapter

5

Supply and Demand of Fund according to the Need of Fishermen

Introduction

A field study was conducted with the help of an appropriate questionnaire. Out of the 1200 sample fishermen, 600 sample fishermen from inland fisheries and an equal number from marine fisheries sector are contacted for this purpose. The sample district has been divided into 3 sub-divisions namely Berhampur, Chatrapur and Bhanjanagar and one NAC (Notified Area Council) such as Gopalpur.

District Level Default Borrowers

An attempt has been made in this chapter to examine the demand and supply of credit to the fishermen of the sample district and the resulting credit gap along with the methods, adopted by the sample fishermen of Ganjam to meet the gap. Table 5.1 reveal that out of 22 Blocks and 1 NAC (Gopalpur) the number of sample borrowers are 1200, number of defaulters are 690 which is 58% per cent. Out of which 408 are defaulters belong to marine sector and 282 belong to inland sector. The number of defaulters in marine sector are 68% and in Inland sector 47%. In marine sector the number of defaulters is high in Ganjam Block and Gopalpur NAC with 82.20 per cent and 82.85 per cent respectively. The number of defaulters is lowest in Chikiti block belongs with 27 defaulters which constitute 33.33 per cent. In Inland sector, the

Table 5.1. District Level Default Borrowers in Different Blocks & NAC Gopalpur

Sl. No.	Block		Marine Sector	Inland Sector	Total
1	2		3	4	5
1.	Rangailunda	B	76	38	114
		D	27	25	52
		%	35.53	65.78	45.61
2.	Kukudakhandi	B	—	54	54
		D	—	20	20
		%	—	37.03	37.03
3.	Chikiti	B	81	69	150
		D	27	23	50
		%	33.33	33.33	33.33
4.	Patrapur	B	—	37	37
		D	—	26	26
		%	—	70.27	70.27
5.	Chatrapur	B	80	32	112
		D	54	11	65
		%	62.5%	34.37	58.04
6.	Khallikote	B	—	16	16
		D	—	7	7
		%	—	43.75	43.75
7.	Purusotampur	B	—	14	14
		D	—	6	6
		%	—	42.85	42.85
8.	Kodala	B	—	39	39
		D	—	15	15
		%	—	38.46	38.46
9.	Hinjilicut	B	—	17	17
		D	—	5	5
		%	—	29.41	29.41

1	2		3	4	5
10.	Ganjam	B	118	11	129
		D	97	4	101
		%	82.20	36.36	78.29
11.	Polsara	B	—	13	13
		D	—	4	4
		%	—	30.76	30.76
12.	Kabisurya Nagar	B	—	17	17
		D	—	6	6
		%	—	35.29	35.29
13.	Bhanjanagar	B	—	16	16
		D	—	7	7
		%	—	43.75	43.75
14.	Belaguntha	B	—	66	66
		D	—	37	37
		%	—	56.06	56.06
15.	Jaganath Prasad	B		12	12
		D	—	5	5
		%	—	41.67	41.67
16.	Buguda	B	—	18	18
		D	—	10	10
		%	—	55.55	55.55
17.	Aska	B	—	34	34
		D	—	21	21
		%	—	61.76	61 76
18.	Seragada	B	—	14	14
		D	—	8	8
		%	—	57.14	57.14
19.	Dharakote	B	—	12	12
		D	—	4	4
		%	—	33.33	33.33

1	2		3	4	5
20.	Sorada	B	—	11	11
		D	—	5	5
		%	—	45.45	45.55
21.	Digapahandi	B	—	9	9
		D	—	5	5
		%	—	55.56	55.56
22.	Sanakhemundi	B	—	31	31
		D	—	15	15
		%	—	48.39	48.39
23.	Gopalpur	B	245	20	265
		D	203	13	216
		%	82.85	65	81.50
	Total	B	600	600	1200
		D	408	282	690
		%	68	47	58

B = Borrower D = Defaulter % = Percentage.
Source : Compiled from the questionnaire.

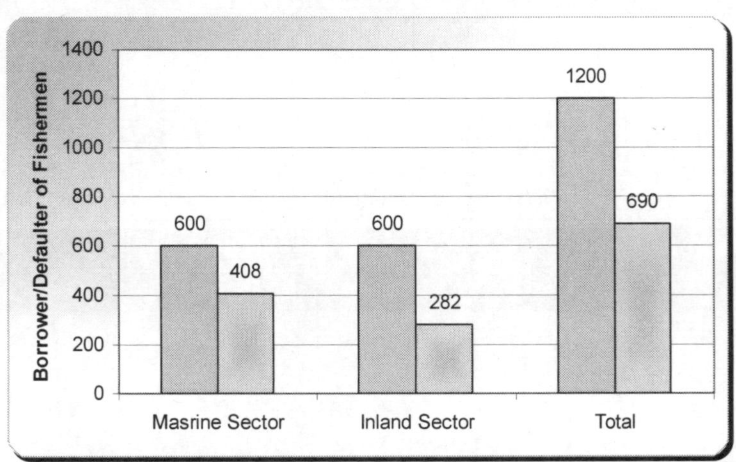

Fig. 5.1 Borrower/Defaulter fishermen in Ganjam district

number of defaulters are highest in Rangelunda (65.78%) and lowest in Hinjilicut with (29.41%). Gopalpur NAC stands first in relation to the number of defaulters i.e., 216 (81.50%). The highest number of defaulters belong to marine sector, because of the fact that they are illiterate.

Demand, Supply and Credit-gap on the Basis of Sex

Out of 1200 sample fishermen, number of male fishermen is quiet higher than fisherwomen. This is shown in the Table 5.2.

Table 5.2. Sex wise demand supply and credit gap in Canjain district

(Rs. in thousand)

Sample		Marine		
		Demand	Supply	Gap
Male	552	17,92,547	12,67,976	5,24,571
%	92			
Female	48	1,01,616	79,198	22,418
%	8			
Total	600	18,94,163	13,47,174	5,46,989
Sample		**Inland**		
		Demand	**Supply**	**Gap**
Male	486	22,000,98	17,11,739	4,88,359
%	81			
Female	114	2,67,102	2,23,473	43,629
%	19			
Total	600	24,67,200	19,35,212	5,31,988
Sample		**Total**		
		Demand	**Supply**	**Gap**
Male	1,038	39,92,645	29,79,715	10,12.930
%	87			
Female	162	3,68,718	3,02,671	66,047
%	13			
Total	1,200	43,61,363	32,82,386	10,78,977

% = Percentage

Source: Compiled from the questionnaire.

Table 5.2 reveals that number of male fisherman borrowers is as high as 1038 (87%) and female fisherwoman borrowers is as low as 162 (13%). The number of male fishermen is high in marine sector which is 552, and have been low in Inland sector which is 486. Per capita credit gap of male fisherman is Rs. 975 where as per capita gap of fisherwoman is Rs. 407. It can be concluded that fisherwomen are utilizing the loan properly and they should be encouraged by different banks, government so that the socio-economic development of the fishing community can be possible. It is observe that the supply of fund is 75 per cent of the amount demanded by the fishennen community.

Credit-gap on the Basis of Literacy

Education plays an important role towards the socio-economic development of the fishermen community. 1200 sample fishermen reveal that percentage of illiterate fishermen is high in comparison to literate fishermen which is clearly reflected in the Table 5.3.

Table 5.3. Demand, Supply and Credit Gap on the Basis of Literacy in Ganjam District

(Rs. in thousand)

Sample		Marine		
		Demand	Supply	Gap
Literate	54	2,09,466	1,78,544	30,922
Percentage	9			
Illiterate	546	16,84,697	11,68,630	5,16,067
Percentage	91	—	—	—
Total	600	18,94,163	13,47,174	5,46,989

Sample		Inland (Rs. in Thousand)		
		Demand	Supply	Gap
Literate	156	6,20,568	5,67,489	53,079
Percentage	26			
Illiterate	444	18,46,632	13,67,723	4,78,909
Percentage	74			
Total	600	24,67,200	19,35,212	5,31,988

Sample		Total (Rs. in Thousand)		
		Demand	Supply	Gap
Literate	210	8,30,034	7,46,033	84,001
Percentage	17.5			
Illiterate	990	3,5,31,329	25,36,353	9,94,976
Percentage	82.5			
Total	1200	43,61,363	32,82,386	10,78.977

Source: Compiled from the questionnaire

Table 5.3 reveals that number of literate sample fishermen is 210 (17.5%), whereas the number of illiterate fishermen is 990 (82.5%). The per capita credit gap of literate fishermen is Rs.400 whereas it is as high as Rs. 1,005 for illiterate fisherman. Number of illiterate fishermen in marine sector is 546 which is 91 per cent and literate fishermen in marine sector are 54 which is nine percent. In Inland sector illiterate fishermen's number is 444 (74%) whereas it is 156 (26%) for literate fishermen. The demand for fund in marine sector is Rs. 18,94,163 but the supply of fund is Rs. 13,47,174 and the credit gap is Rs. 5,46,989. But in Inland sector the demand for fund is Rs. 24,67,200, and the supply for fund is Rs. 19,35,212 and credit gap is Rs. 5,31,988. So it can be concluded that lack of education among fishermen is one of the important reasons for being economically backward. They are using the fund in unproductive purpose.

Demand Supply and Credit Gap of Sample Fishermen (Inland Sector) in Ganjam District

Six hundred samples were taken in inland sector of Ganjam district to find out demand, supply and credit gap of the fishermen. This is shown in Table 5.4.

Table 5.4. Demand, Supply and Credit Gap of Sample Fishermen of Inland Sector in Ganjam District

(Rs. lakhs)

Sl. No.	Name of the Sub division/ NAC		Sample	Demand	Supply	Gap
1.	Berhampur	B	198	—	—	—
		D	94	3,86,528	2,10,902	1,75,626
		%	47.48	—	—	—
		R	104	4,27,646	4,27,648	NIL
		%	52.52	—	—	—
	Total			8,14.176	6,38,550	1,75,626
2.	Chatrapur	B	159	—	—	—
		D	58	2,38,395	97,362	1,41,033
		%	36.48	—	—	—
		R	101	4,15,413	4,15,413	NIL
		%	63.52	—	—	—
	Total			6,53,808	5,12,775	1,41,033
3.	Bhanjanagar	B	223	—	—	—
		D	117	4,08,998	2,11,409	1,97,589
		%	52,47	—	—	—
		R	106	5,07,978	5,07,978	NIL
		%	47.53	—	—	—
	Total			9,16,976	7,19,387	1,97,589
4.	Gopalpur	B	20	—	—	—
		D	13	53,340	35,600	17,740
		%	65	—	—	—
		R	7	28,900	28,900	—
		%	35	—	—	—
	Total			82,240	64,500	17,740
	Total	B	600	24,67,200	19,35,212	5,31,988
		D	282	10,87,261	5.55,273	5,31,988
		%	47	—	—	—
		R	318	13,79,939	13,79,939	NIL
		P	53	—	—	—

B = Borrower D = Defaulter % = Percentage R = Repayment

Source: Compiled from the questionnaire.

Table 5.4 reveals that out of 600 sample fishermen 282 are defaulters (47%) and 318 (53%) are the fishermen who have repaid the loan. In Inland sector the total demand for funds is Rs. 24,67,200 the total supply of fund is Rs. 19,35,212 and the gap is Rs. 5,31,988. In Berhampur subdivision the total demand for fund is Rs. 8,14,176 the total supply of fund is Rs. 6,38,550 and credit gap is Rs. 1,75,626. In Chatrapur subdivision the demand for fund is Rs. 6,53,808 the total supply of fund is Rs. 5,12,775 and the credit gap is Rs. 1,41,033. Similarly in Bhanjanagar subdivision the demand for fund is Rs. 9,16,976 the supply of fund is Rs. 7,19,387 and the credit gap is Rs. 1,97,589. In Gopalpur NAC total demand for fund is Rs. 82,240, the total supply of fund is Rs. 64,500 and the credit-gap is Rs. 17,740. So it can be concluded that fishermen in this sector are cautious and are willing to repay the loan in time.

Demand, Supply and Credit Gap of Marine Sector Sample Fishermen in Ganjam District

The demand, supply and credit gap of 600 sample fishermen, in Ganjam district are spread over two subdivisions namely, Berhampur, Chatrapur, and one NAC (Gopalpur). Table 5.5 reveals that out of 600 sample fishermen 408 (68%) are defaulters and 192 (32%) fishermen have repaid the loan. The total demand for fund, is Rs. 18,94,163, the total supply of fund is Rs. 13,47,174 and the gap is Rs. 5,46,989. In Gopalpur NAC the gap is maximum to a tune for Rs. 2,23,195 and Berhampur subdivision records the lowest amount of Rs. 1,43,298. In Berhampur subdivision the total demand for fund is Rs. 4,95,937, the supply of fund is Rs. 3,52,639 and the gap is Rs. 1,43,298. Similarly in Chatrapur the total demand for fund is Rs. 6,25,006, the Supply is Rs. 4,44,510 and the resultant gap is Rs. 1,80,496. In Gopalpur NAC the total demand for fund is Rs. 7,73,220, the total supply of fund is Rs. 5,50,025 and the gap is Rs. 2,23,195.

Table 5.5. Demand, Supply and Credit Gap of Sample Fishermen of Marine Sector in Ganjam District

(Rs. lakh)

Sl. No.	Name of the Sub division/ NAC		Sample	Demand	Supply	Gap
1.	Berhampur	B	157			
		D	54	2,75,849	1,32,551	1,43,298
		%	34			
		R	103	2,2,0,088	2,20,088	NIL
		%	65.61			
		Total		4,95,937	3,52,639	1,43,298
2.	Chatrapur	B	198			
		D	151	4,76,646	2,96,150	1,80,496
		%	76.26			
		R	47	1,48,360	1,48,360	NIL
		%	23,74			
		Total	—	6,25,006	4,44,510	1,80,496
3.	Gopalpur	B	245	—	—	—
		D	203	6,40,584	4,17,389	2,23,195
		%	82.86			
		R	42	1,32,636	1,32,636	NIL
		%	1214	—	—	—
	Total		—	7,73,220	5,50,025	2,23,195
	G. Total	B	600	18,94,163	13,47,174	5,46,989
		D	408	13,93,079	8,46,090	5,46,989
		%	68	—	—	—
		R	192	5,01,084	5,01,084	—
		P	32	—	—	—

B = Borrower D = Defaulter % = Percentage R = Repayment
Source: Compiled from the questionnaire

Demand, Supply and Credit Gap of Funds in Ganjam District

Out of 1200 samples, it is found that the number of defaulters is high in marine sector (408) and low in Inland sector (282) Table 5.6.

Table 5.6. Demand, Supply and Credit-gap of funds in fishery sector of Ganjam district

(Rs. lakh)

Sl. No.	Name of the Sub division/ NAC		Sample Fishermen	Demand	Supply	Gap
1.	Berhampur	B	355	—	—	—
		D	148	6,62,377	3,43,453	3,18,924
		%	41.70	—	—	—
		R	207	647,736	6,47,736	NIL
		%	—	—	—	—
		Total	58.30	13,10,113	9,91,189	3,18,924
2.	Chatrapur	B	357	—	—	—
		D	209	7,15,041	3,93,512	3,21,529
		%	58.55	—	—	—
		R	148	5,63,773	5,63,773	NIL
		%	41.45	—	—	—
		Total		12,78,814	9,57,285	3,21,529
3.	Bhanjanagar	B	223	—	—	—
		D	117	4,08,998	2,11,409	1,97,589
		%	52.47	—	—	—
		R	106	5,07,978	5,07,978	NIL
		%	47.53	—	—	—
		Total		9,16,976	7,19,387	1,97,589
4.	Gopalpur	B	265	—	—	—
		D	216	6,93,924	4,52,989	2,40,935
		%	81.50	—	—	—
		R	49	1,61,536	1,61,536	NIL
		%	1850	—	—	—
		Total		8,55,460	6,14,525	2,40,935
5.	Total	B	1200	43,61,363	32,82,386	10,78,977
		D	690	24,80,340	14,01,363	10,78,977
		%	508	—	—	—
		R	510	18,81,023	18,81,023	—
		%	42	—	—	—

B = Borrower D = Defaulter % = Percentage R = Repayment
Source: Complied from the questionnaire.

Table 5.6 takes into account the total fishery sector of Ganjam district. Out of the sample 1200 fishermen, 690 (58%) fishermen are defaulters and 510 (42%) sample fishermen have repaid the loan. The total demand for fund is Rs. 43,61,363, total supply of fund is Rs. 32,82,386 and the credit-gap is Rs. 10,78,977. The number of defaulters in marine sector are 408 and in inland sector are 282. The demand for fund in Berhampur subdivision is Rs. 13,10,113, the supply of fund is Rs. 9,91,189 and the credit-gap is Rs. 3,18,924. The demand for fund in Chatrapur Subdivision is Rs. 12,78,814, the supply of fund is Rs. 9,57,285 and the credit-gap is Rs. 3,21,529. In Bhanjanagar, the demand for fund is Rs. 9,16,976, the supply of fund is 7,19,387 and the credit-gap is Rs. 1,97,589. But in Gopalpur NAC the total demand for fund is Rs. 8.55,460, the supply of fund is Rs. 6,14.525 and the credit gap is Rs. 2,40,935. From the observation it is found that the no of defaulters in Gopalpur are 216, which is the highest. Similarly the credit gap is also the highest in Chatrapur Rs. 3,21,529.

Methods of Meeting Credit-gap

Out of the 1200 sample fishermen, 690 were victimised by the credit gap for carrying out their operation successfully. They were compelled to make good the deficit (credit-gap), by various method. The number of defaulters are reported in Table 5.7 and Fig. 5.2.

The pie chart shown in Fig. 5.2 clearly shows that out of the 690 defaulters 54 (8%) pledged gold, 97 (14%) defaulters mortgage land, 57 (8%) defaulters mortgage boat 32 (5%) defaulters mortgaged house and 450 (65%) defaulters have brought loan from non institutional agencies. It is quite clear that the non institutional agencies play an important role towards providing finance to the needy fishermen.

Demand Supply and Credit Gap of Funds by the Non-institutional Agencies to Fishermen of Ganjam District

The defaulter borrower fishermen have opted for finance from non-institutional agencies which is depicted in Table 5.8.

Table 5.7. Credit-Gap Affected Borrower Fishermen in Ganjam district

(In. No)

Sl. No.	Subdivision NAC		Pledged Gold	Mortagaged land	Mortgaged of Boat	Mortgaged of house	Non-institutional Agency	Total
1.	Berhampur	B	6	35	19	8	80	148
		%	4.06	23.65	12.84	5.40	54.05	100
2.	Chatrapur	B	11	27	11	10	150	209
		%	5.26	12.93	5.26	4.78	71.77	100
3.	Bhanjanagar	B	35	33	05	09	35	117
		%	29.91	28.22	4.27	7.69	29.91	100
4.	Gopalpur	B	02	02	22	05	183	216
		%	0.92	0.92	10.19	2.32	85.65	100
	Total	B	54	97	57	32	450	690
		%	8	14	8	5	65	100

B = Borrower   % = Percentage

Source : Compiled from the questionnaire.

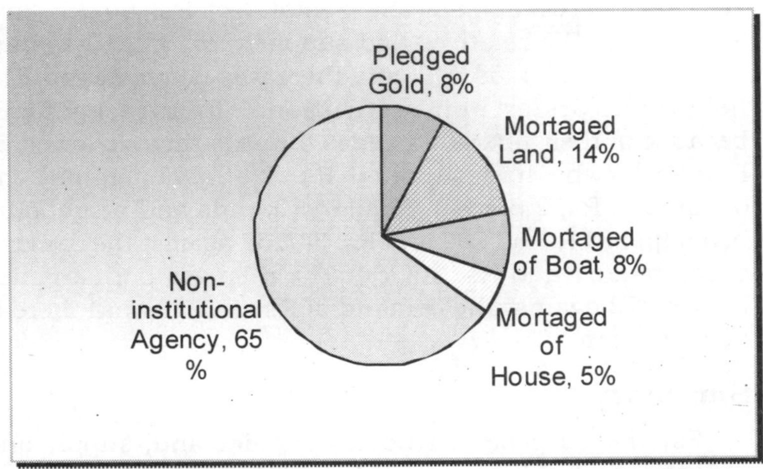

Fig. 5.2. Credit Gap effected Borrower in Ganjan District

Table 5.8. Demand Supply and Credit Gap of Funds by the Non-institutional Agency to Fishermen of Ganjam District

(Rs. lakh)

Sl. No.	Name of the Non-institutional agencies	Demand	Supply	Gap	% tage
1.	Sahukars	3,57,252	3,54,936	2,316	99.35
2.	Landlords	2,85,343	2,82,891	2,452	99.14
3.	Friends	64,251	62,297	1,954	96.99
4.	Relatives	58,212	58,212	—	100
5.	Neighbours	36,254	34,167	2,087	94.24
	Total	8,01,312	7,92,503	8,809	98.90

Source: Compiled from the questionnaire

Table 5.8 shows that the largest supplier of finance were Sahukar who had supplied Rs. 3,54,936 against the demand of Rs. 3,57,252 followed by landlords who had supplied Rs. 2,82,891 against the demand of Rs. 2,85,343. Similarly friends and neighbours had supplied Rs. 62,297 and Rs. 34,167 against the demand of Rs. 64,251 and Rs. 36,254. The relatives had supplied Rs. 58,212 against the demand of Rs. 58,212, and there was no credit gap. The fishermen prefer non-institutional finance ageneies because of their liberal attitudes towards them followed by landlords who had supplied Rs. 2,82,891 against the demand of Rs. 2.85.343. Similarly friends and neighbours had supplied Rs. 62,297 and Rs. 34,167 against the demand of Rs. 64,251 and Rs. 36,254. The relatives had supplied Rs. 58,212 against the demand of Rs. 58,212, and there is no credit gap.

Summary

For the purpose of studying the demand, supply and credit gap of fund, a sample of 600 from marine sector and 600 from inland sector were taken into account which were selected at random. The sample district Ganjam had been divided into three subdivisions such as Berhampur, Chatrapur & Bhanjanagar and one NAC such as Gopalpur.

Table 5.1 clearly shows that at the district level out of 1200 sample fishermen of defaulters were 690 (58%) and the number of non-defaulting fishermen were 510 (42%). Among the defaulters 408 (68%) belong to marine sector and 282 (47%) belong to inland sector The highest number of defaulters in marine sector were found in Gopalpur covering 82.85 per cent and in inland sector at Rangaillunda totaling 65.78 per cent.

Similarly the demand, supply and credit gap on the basis of sex revealed that in marine sector the number of male fishermen borrower is 1038. Per capita credit gap of male fishermen was Rs. 975 and fever fisherwomen was Rs. 407. So it can be concluded that fisherwomen were utilized the loan amount properly than their male counterparts. Further, the supply of fund was 75 per cent against of the total amount demanded. The credit gap on the basis of literacy shows that literate fishermen in marine sector was 54 (9%) and in inland sector it is 156. Similarly the number of illiterate fishermen in marine sector is 546 (91%) and in inland sector it is 444 (74%). Hence, the number of literate sample fishermen are 210 (17.5%) and illiterate fishermen are 990 (82.5%). The per capita gap of literate fishermen was Rs. 400 but it was as high as Rs. 1005 for illiterate fishermen. So it can be concluded that the illiterate borrowers were utilizing the fund in an unproductive way.

In inland sector the demand for fund was Rs. 24,67,200 whereas the supply of fund was Rs. 19,35,212 and the credit gap was Rs. 5,31,988. The number of defaulters were 282 (47%) and non-defaulters are 318 (53%)

In marine sector the demand for fund was Rs. 18,94,163 the supply of fund was Rs. 13,47,174 and the credit gap is Rs. 5,46,989. Number of defaulter fishermen were 408 (68%), and 192 had repaid the loan.

In the sample district of Ganjam the demand for fund was Rs. 43,61,367, the total supply of fund was Rs. 32,82,386 and the gap was Rs. 10,78,977. The number of defaulters were 690 (58%) and number of repayers was 510 (42%). Out of 1200 sample fishermen, 690 were victimized by the credit gap. To overcome the deficit amount, 8 per cent fishermen have pleged gold, 14 per cent mortaged land; 8 per cent mortaged boat; 5 per cent mortaged houses and 65 per cent have opted for finance from non-institutional agencies. It is observed that non-institutional financial agencies have supplied nearly 99 per cent of the total amount demanded by the fishermen community.

Chapter 6

Socio-economic Condition of Fishermen : An Analysis

Introduction

Socio-economic conditions of fishermen in the district of Ganjam are taken for analysis. This chapter deals with various reasons responsible for their socio-economic conditions. For marine fishing sector and inland fishing sector 600 samples were taken. In all, 1200 samples were taken from the were district consisting of three subdivisions i.e., Berhampur, Chatrapur and Bhanjanagar and one Notified Area Council (NAC), namely Gopalpur by an appropriate questionnaire. There were various reasons relating to socio-economic development of fishermen such as finance, marketing, fishing equipment etc. which were also examined in this chapter. Analysis have been made in this chapter from different angles touching upon age, sex, caste, etc to have a clear picture regarding the socio-economic conditions of the fishermen in the district of Ganjam at borrowers level.

Lack of Infrastructure Facilities is an Obstacle for Development of Fishermen in Ganjam District

Development of a country depends very much on the availability of its infrastructural facilities. Without a sound infrastructural base a country cannot develop its economy. These infrastructural facilities include various transportation, communication, economical and social overhead, such as energy (coal, oil, electricity), irrigation, banking, finance, insurance, science and technology and social overheads such as education, health and Ingiene.

In the fishery sector of the district, Ganjam, the fishermen are deprived of the basic infrastructure facilities such as fishing jetties, harbour, cold storage, capital, transport, marketing, crafts and gears. This can be illustrated in Table 6.1 and Fig. 6.1 and Fig 6.2.

Table 6.1. Non-availability of Infrastructure Facilities in the District Ganjam

(In No.)

Sl. No.	Non-availability of infrastructure facilities	No. of Samples	Percentage
1	Fishing jetties	84	7%
2.	Harbour	48	4%
3.	Cold storage	108	9%
4	Finance	480	40%
5	Marketing	144	12%
6	Transportation	108	9%
7	Crafts and Gears	2.28	19%
	Total	1200	100%

%= Percentage

Source: Compiled from the Questionnaire.

The pie chart (Fi. 6.2) clearly shows the different reasons responsible for the degradation of financial condition of fishermen community in the Ganjam district. Seven per cent of sample respondents were of the view that lack of fishing jetties is a reason. Lack of harbour in the locality for which ships cannot arrive is another cause for four per cent of fishermen. Furthermore, nine per cent complained about the non-availibily of cold storage due to which fishes cannot be stored and gets decomposed easily. fourteen per cent of fishermen complained poor quality marketing and nine per cent complained about transportation, and 19 per cent talked about the non-availability of crafts and gears. But 40 per cent of the respondents complained about insufficient finance, for the cause of their poverty. Most of them live below poverty line. They simply make a hand to mouth living and hence could not afford to purchase needful articles of fishing.

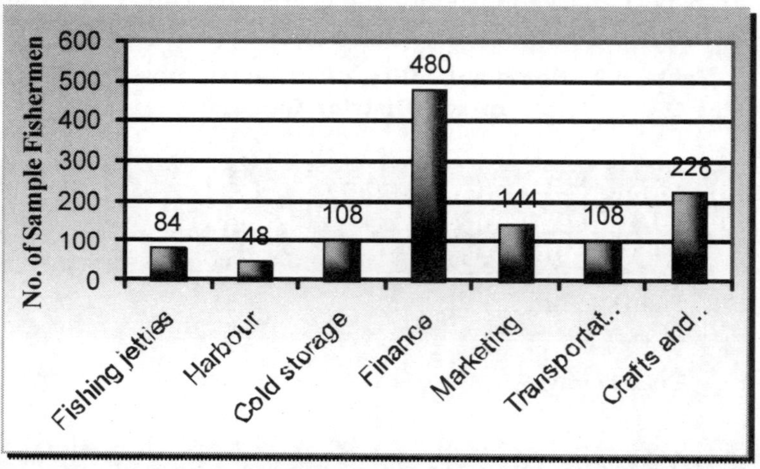

Fig. 6.1. Non-Availability of Infrastructure Facilities in the District Ganjam

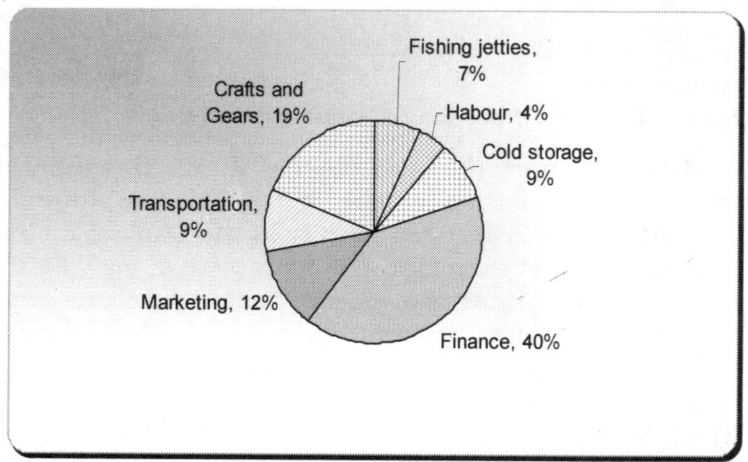

Fig. 6.2. Non-Availability of Infrastructure Facilities in the District Ganjam

Seasonal Fishing Creates Problem for Economic Development of Fishermen

It is observed that sea fishing is not a regular business of the fishermen. They go on for fishing for only 169 (46%) days average in a year and that too they are not fishing in the deep sea, where it can fetch a good catch. It clearly shows that the fishermen community of Ganjam is under developed and backward both financially and socially and need Government boosting resulting in quiet a sizeable amount of profit. As they are handicapped by different modern fishing equipments they could only enter 6 to 8 km (maximum) in to deep sea and fishing was mostly done in the sea. Hence, it is found that fishing does not contribute financially much to their families It is also found that they are engaged elsewhere. The reason for poor performance of fish landings of the district is due to low rate of mechanization of crafts and inadequate infrastructure facilities for marine fishing.

Due to low income, some are shifting to other occupations such as cultivation, daily wages, small retail business. This is shown in Table 6.2; Fig, 6.5 and Fig. 6.4.

The pie chart (Fig. 6.4) shows that 18 per cent sample fishermen were of the opinions that rough sea and bad weather conditions prevent them from fishing through-out the year. On an average only 169 days is available for fishing. From April to August due to rough sea they could not enter the sea for fishing. The sea coast is frequently hit by the cyclone many times a year preventing them from fishing. Hence, it became difficult to depend on fishing as a profession, 42 per cent respondent were of the opinion that lack of modern fishing equipments like BLC's IBE or OBM engine, and invasion of trawlers etc. had hampered the fish collection. They use traditional catamaran, which was confined to 3-4 kilometres from the shore, so deep sea fishing is not possible. Nineteen per cent of sample fishermen were of the view that Andhra trawler invade the coastal area of the district and carry a huge quantity of fish with them. Small fishes were hit by trawlers thus

Table 6.2. A Classification of Causes for Having Bad Catch in Marine Sector of Ganjam District

Maximum catch	Minimum catch	No. of fishing days in a year		Reasons for not having good catch	No. of Samples	% age
October	April	Jan	21	(*a*) Rough sea and bad	106	18
November	May	Feb	14	weather		
December	June	March	12	conditions, floods		
January	July	April	09	& cyclones		
February	Aug	May	08	(*b*) Non-availability		
March	Sept	June	07	of modern fishing	258	42
		July	09	equipments like		
		Aug.	10	mechanized boats		
		Sept.	11	and trawlers etc.		
		Oct.	21	(*c*) Invasion of coastal	114	19
		Nov.	24	area by Andhra		
		Dec.	23	trawlers		
				(*d*) Missile test by	45	8
		Total	169	army unit at		
		days		Gopalpur		
				(*e*) Medical problems	39	7
				(*f*) Bad Luck	38	6
				Total	600	100

Source: Compiled from the questionnaire

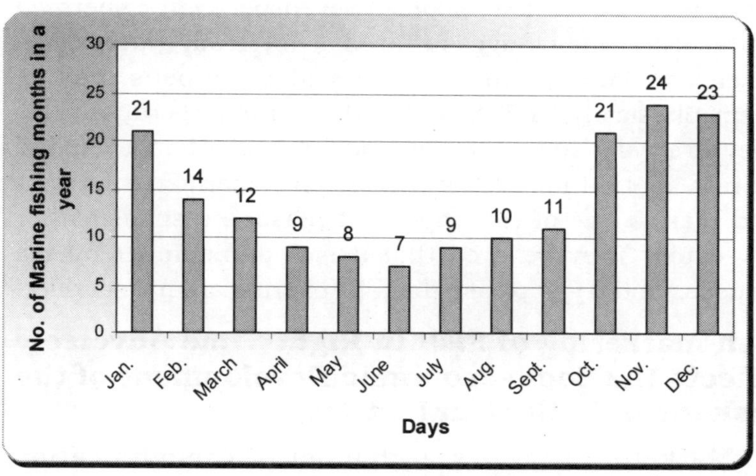

Fig. 6.3. Nos. of Fishing Days.

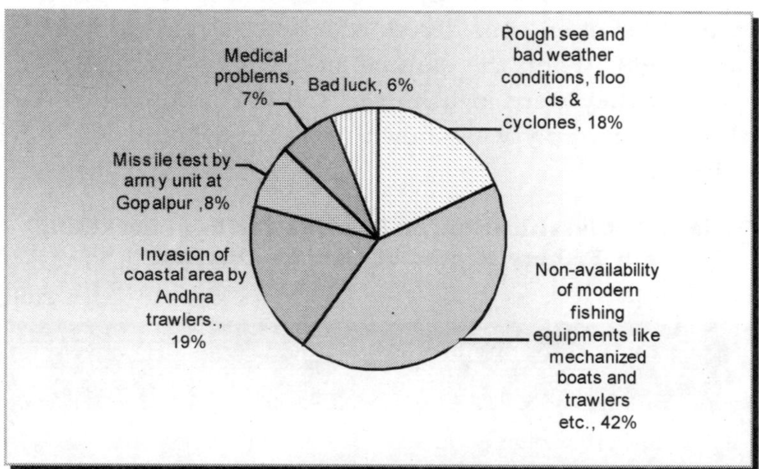

Fig. 6.4. Causes of bad catches.

reducing their catch to a greater extent. Eight per cent fishermen especially in Gopalpur NAC were of the view that army units at Golabandh is conducting missile test in Gopalpur on a regular basis. During their operation fishermen were prohibited from entering the sea for fear of loss of life, making them to sit idle during the operation days. It reduces their earning leaving them in a precarious stage with a very low income. Seven per cent fishermen states that they have suffered a lot from water-born diseases. Some minor accidents also happens making them physically unfit to carry the fishing operations. As they are very poor, they are not in a position to spend money for treatment, Six percent of fishermen said that bad luck is one of the important reasons responsible for low catch. They believed that it is a punishment by sea Goddess and try to please them by offering animal sacrifice.

Non-marketing of Fish in Right Time Adversely Affects the Socio-economic Development of the Fishermen in Ganjam District

Marketing provides a channel of communication between the producer and the consumer who ultimately determine the price. Analysis of marketing is important because it is often considered to be a constraint to fishery development. When the sample subjects were questioned as to why they were in a him to sell the products at the earliest, their reply was shown in Table 6.3 and Fig. 6.5 and Fig. 6.6.

Table 6.3. Classification of Reasons for Non-marketing in Fishery Sector of Ganjam District.

(In No)

Sl. No.	Reasons for non-marketing	Total	%
1.	Lack of storage facility	108	9
2.	Distress sale	145	12
3.	Lack of transportation	108	9
4.	Interference by middlemen, brokers	239	20
5.	Lack of organization	120	10
6.	Lack of institutional finance	480	40
	Total	1200	100

Source: Compiled from the Questionnaire.

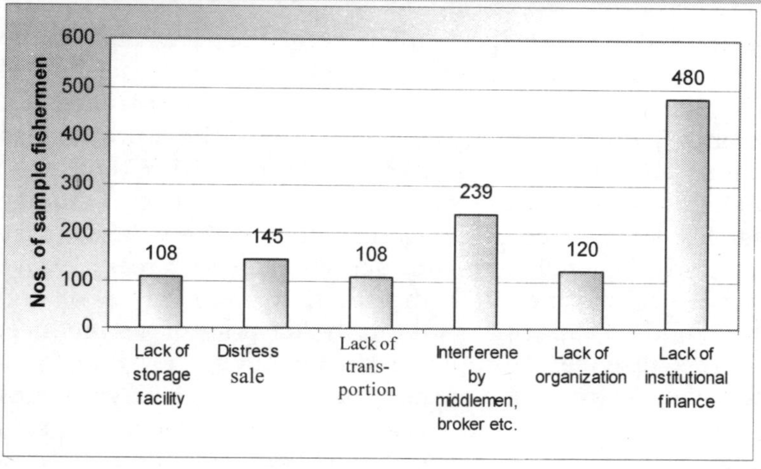

Fig. 6.5. Reasons for Non-marketing of Fish

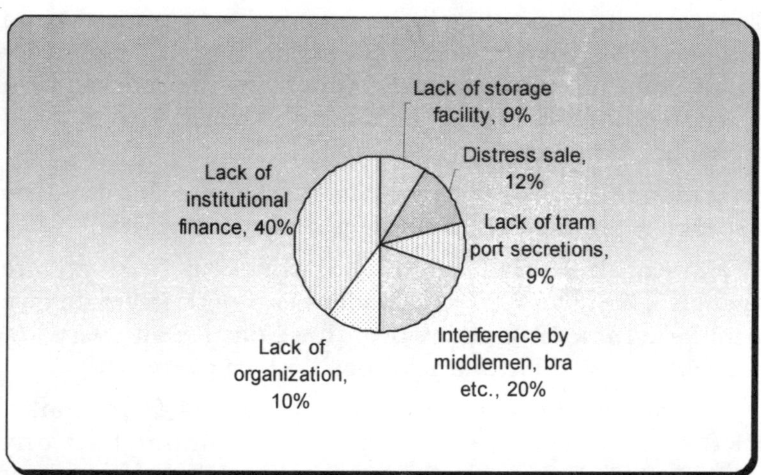

Fig. 6.6. Reasons of Non-marketing of fish by Percentage.

The Piehart (Fig. 6.6) clearly reveals that marketing was greatly hampered due to intervention of intermediaries like sahukars, money, lenders etc. Twenty per cent, fishermen of the opinion that a large number of intermediaries existing between fishermen and the consumers. These middlemen claimed a good amount of margin and thus reduce the return of the fishermen to a great extent. Forty per cent here of the view that in the absence of adequate institutional finance, fishermen of the district had to come under the clutches of trader and money-lender. Hence, they had to sell their produce to these people at unfavourable terms. Nine per cent fishermen were of the view that in the absence of storage facility such as cold storage facilities in the villages, they are forced to sell their produce at a cheaper rate. Twelve per cent fishermen said that as they were very poor and thus had no capacity to wait for better price of his produce. In the absence of proper credit facilities, they had to go for even distress sale of their out put to the village money lenders-cum-traders at a cheaper price. Nine per cent said that in the absence of proper road transportation facilities in the rural area, fishermen could not reach nearby markets to sell their produce at a fair price. Hence they preferred to sell their produce at the village market itself. Ten per cent opine that lack of collective organization on the part of fishermen lead them to this position. So a very small amount of fishes were brought to the market by a huge number of small fishermen leading to a high transportation cost.

Finance is closely related to marketing. For this the fishermen are divided in to three broad categories.

Firstly these fishermen who took loan from private agencies, *sahukars*, money-lenders etc. were forced to give a major chunk of their catch to these parties at a very low prices. Hence, their financial position was very bad.

Secondly, the fishermen who got loans from banks, RRB's, co-operative societies etc. seldom had any interference. Hence, they were free to sell their catch at a reasonable price and thus their financial position was quiet satisfactory.

Thirdly, some fishermen do not take any loans. Moreover, they had some parental property, income from agriculture, dealt with Kiaffulla cultivation which fetched them a high price. These fishermen were financially strong and were not in a huary to sell their catch. They were engaged in selling their fishes to neighbouring

States, and they also possessed boat, net at then disposal. These fishermen also used important preservation technique.

Again selling is an art. It requires the following important qualities:

(*a*) Sound health

(*b*) Appearance

(*c*) Pleasant voice

(*d*) Alertness

(*e*) Confidence

(*f*) Enthusiasm

(*g*) Good manners

(*h*) Integrity.

Coming to the samples, their activities were analysed against the qualities and characteristics mentioned above. The Nolias enter the sea and when they returned they used to divide the whole catch into eight equal parts. The six 'Nolia's used to take six parts and the rest two portions were given to the owners of boat and net as their rent. It was also found the whole group took the responsibility for fishing and in some cases it was found that in each group there was a leader taking responsibility of the trade. Five member used to take their own portion of their catch as wages and it was found that in some cases, group could not last long and there were many changes in grouping. In this way it was found that most of the fishermen never took responsibilities, but had to content with the portion of their catch as their wages. But in some cases the fishermen who owned his own boat and net employ some fishermen in inland fishing and has to give them their own portion of the catch. In this way there were distinct ways of business as far as the subjects were concerned. They were all divided into three group:

Group A – Superior,

Group B – Average and

Group C – Inferior.

A Superior Group– They are never in a hurry to dispose of the catch but sold them at their own terms and .conditions because they are financially viable as they had a good source of income from other sources (Kiafulla business). They used preservation techniques like canning, sun-drying, dry-salting, brining, smoking, pickling. These are popularly known as curing. So their income was more of less stable and is rewarding to them.

B. Average Group– Average fishermen are those who have their own boats and nets and some had to get them on rent basis But they are not financially as strong as Group A.

C. Interior Group– These fishermen have no boats and nets and have to borrow them from others and have to pay their rent at the end of the day. They are in a hurry to sell the catch on the sea. They sell their produce to some brokers, middle-men even if the bargain is against there will.

In this way their groups are divided as superior, average and inferior.

Difficulties faced by Fishermen while obtaining Bank Finance

Banks play a major part in providing finance to fishermen. Table 6.4, and Fig. 6.7-6.8 show the obstacles difficulties faced by the fishermen while obtaining finance from the bank.

Table 6.4. Difficulties Faced by Fishermen of District in Obtaining Bank Finance

(in No)

Sl. No.	Obstacles for getting finance	No of sample fishermen	Percent
1.	Attitude of Bank Officials	390	33
2.	Security	404	34
3.	Formalities of Bank	137	11
4.	Middle-men's Interference	127	10
5.	Ignorance of law	142	12
	Total	1200	100

Source: Compiled from the questionnaire.

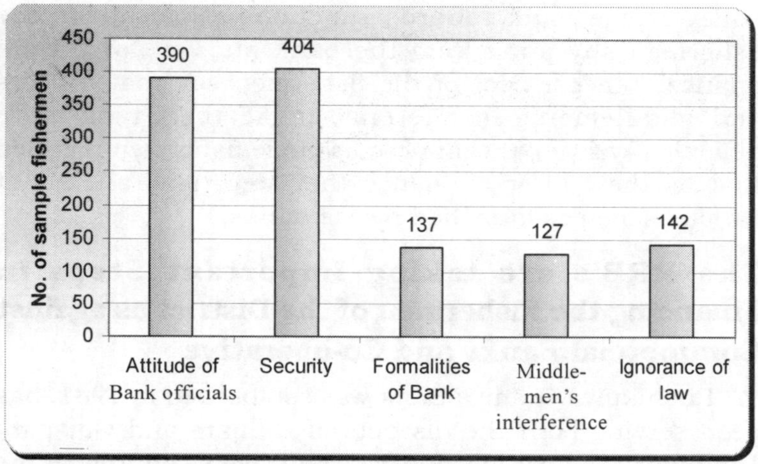

Fig. 6.7. Obstacles for Getting Finance (in Nos).

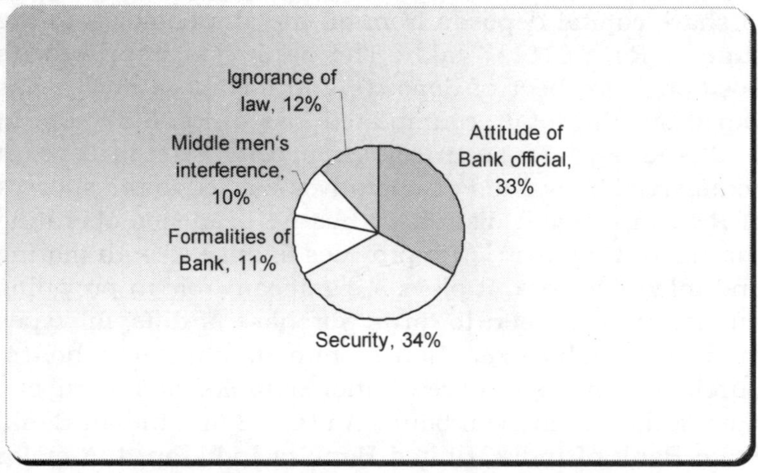

Fig. 6.8. Obstacles forgetting Finance in percentage

Table 6.4 reveals that 34 per cent sample fishermen were of the view that the not so liberal policy of the bank like asking for security like *patta,* pledging gold, etc. plays a major hurdle. Thirty-three per cent were the view that the high headness of bank officials was the main obstacle. Towards sanctioning of loan to the poor fishermen 1 per cent of the sample fishermen said that due to the rigid policy of the bank towards sanctioning loan made the fishermen shy away from the bank and opt for private finance. Ten per cent of the fishermen say that brokers and middlemen's interference make their task more difficult. Twellve per cent of the sample fishermen revealed that as they illiterate, hence they were ignorant about various schemes launched by the banks.

The RRB's are taking Important Steps in Financing the Fishermen of the District as against Commercial Banks and Co-operative

Rushikulya Gramya Bank was established in 1981, has been serving both the districts of Ganjam and Gajapati. The bank has been playing a pivotal role in improving the standard of living of rural masses of both the districts. The bank was received restructuring assistance in the from of share capital deposits from all the shareholders to the tune of Rs. 1815.27 lakh. The bank has improved its position in respect of deposits and advances and it has wiped out the total accumulated loss of Rs. 8.37 core in 2002-03 and is running on profit. The failure of commercial banks and co-operatives has led to the success of RRB in Ganjam district. It has 64 branches operating throughout the district. It provides finance to both marine and inland sectors. It plays a significant role in providing finance to fishermen towards purchase of different types of nets, mechanized boats, non-mechanised boats, purchase of fish sheed, renovation of tanks, marketing etc. Among the commercial banks Andhra Bank, Indian Bank, State Bank of India, United Bank of India are the major banks lending to the fishermen of the district. The Co-operative Banks have not been able to perform their job quiet satisfactorily and are incurring heavy losses. This is shown in Tables 6.5, 6.6 and Fig. 6.9.

Table 6.5 reveals that the district level sample defaulters were 690 (58%). The rate of defaulting borrowers are high in co-operative sector with 42 (89%). While the least defaulter lies with Regional Rural Banks with 170 (34%). The least defaulters were found in Berhampur subdivision 44 (25%). The percentage of defaulters in commercial bank is 478 (12%). The number of defaulters in Gopalpur NAC is the higest 142 (86%) and lowest in Berhampur subdivision with 98 borrowers (57%). The defaulters number is high in Co-operative Banks because of the inability of the Co-operative Banks to collect the loan from the borrowers Disbursement of credit is also not done properly by these Banks.

Table 6.5. Bankwise Classification of Defaulter Fishermen in Ganjam District

(In No)

Sl. No.	Sub-division/ NAC		Commercial Banks	RRBs	Co-operatives	Total
1.	Berhampur	B	172	174	9	355
		D	98	44	6	148
		%	57	25	67	42
2.	Bhanjanagar	B	117	102	14	233
		D	84	25	8	117
		%	72	24	57	52
3.	Chatrapur	B	207	135	15	357
		D	154	43	12	209
		%	74	32	80	59
4.	Gopalpur-NAe	B	164	82	19	265
		D	142	58	16	216
		%	86	70	84	81
5.	Total	B	660	493	47	1200
		D	478	170	42	690
		%	72	34	89	58

B = Borrower D = Defaulter % = Percentage

Source: Compiled from the questionnaire

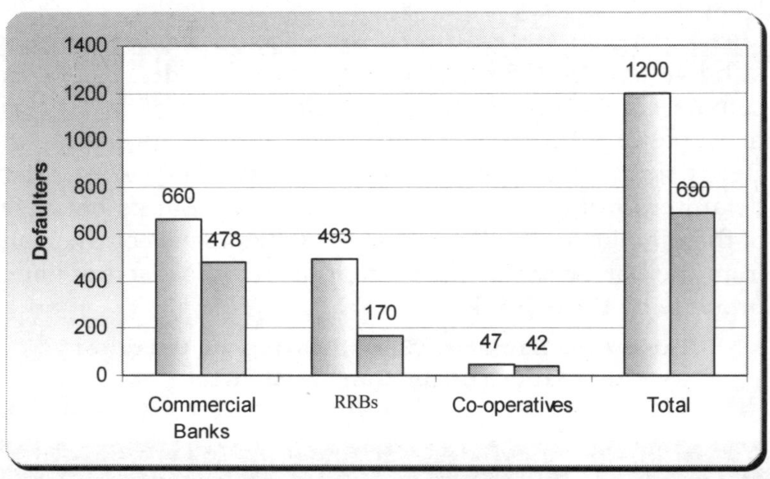

Fig. 6.9. Bankwise defaulters

Different banks have provided finance to 1200 sample fishermen. The amount of finance is provided by different banks in the district are shown in Table 6.6.

Table 6.6. Classification of Finance made by Different Banks in Ganjam District

(Rs. Lakhs)

Sector		RRBs	Commercial Banks	Co-operatives	Total Supply
Marine	S	7,14,002	5,79,285	53,887	13,47,174
	%	53	43	4	100
Inland	S	7,93,437	9,09,550	2,32,225	19,35,212
	%	41	47	12	100
Total	S	15,07,439	14,88,835	2,86,112	32,82,386
	%	47	45	8	100

S = Supply of money % = Percentage.

Source: Compiled from the questionnaire.

From Table 6.6 it is clear that RRBs had provided finance to a tune of Rs. 15,07,439 (47%), Commercial banks had provided Rs. 14,88,835 (45%), and Co-operatives had supplied Rs. 2,86,112 (8%).

Traditional Methods used by Fishermen Hampers their Economic Development

Depending upon environmental conditions different types of fishing gears are being operated in different parts of the district. In the district maximum catch comes from non-mechanised fishing boats. The number of motorised boats are less than non-motorised boats in the district. A number of motorised boats is being operated in Prayagi but traditional catamaran boats are being operated in New-Golabandha, Reekatteru and Sonepur. In Katiagarh fish landing centre, however, a number of non-motorised boats is being operated.

A fishing gear is a device used to catch fish in commercial fishing. Chief among them are the following types of gears and their mode of operation : Nets (netting), hooks and line (lining), traps (centrapping), spears and harpoon (spearing). Netting is responsible in the fishery sector as 90 per cent of fishing is done by this method. The different types of crafts are used for this purpose. The main drawback of fishing, especially in marine sector is that the fishermen with these old methods of crafts and gears fail to enter into the deep sea and rivers where there is abundant supply of fish. In marine sector mainly off-shore fishing is carried on, where catch is gradually decreasing year after year. Table 6.7 and Fig. 6.10 and 6.11 show the ownership of coaft and gears of fishermen in Ganjan district.

Table 6.7. Ownership of craft and gears of fishermen in Ganjam district

(In No)

Sl. No.	Operation of crafts and gears	No. of fishermen	%
1.	No boat	876	72
2.	Traditional boat	105	9
3.	Ordinary net	32	3
4.	Nylon net	91	8
5.	Motorised boat	96	8
	Total	1,200	100

Source: Compiled from the questionnaire.

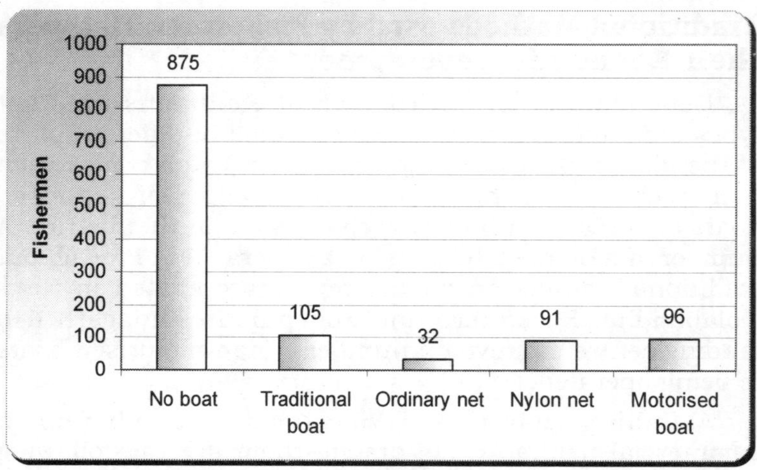

Fig. 6.10. Ownership of Crafts & Gears of Fishermen in Numbers in Ganjan district.

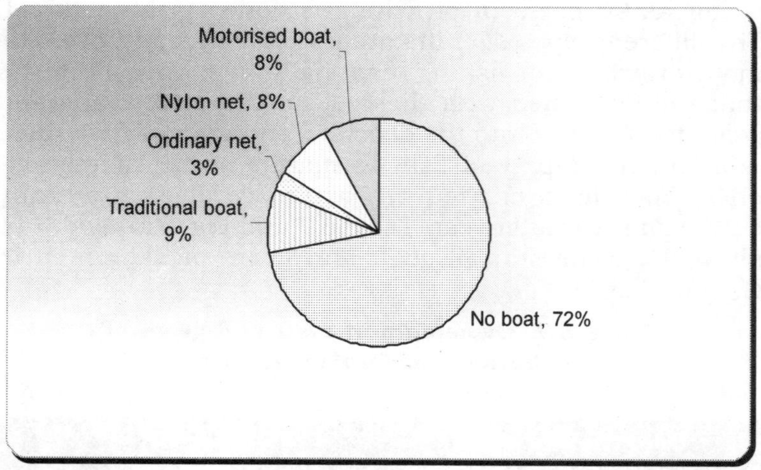

Fig. 6.11. Ownership of craft and gears of fishermen in percentage in Ganjan district

It reveals from the pie chart (Fig. 6.11) that 72 per cent of fishermen have no boats. Three per cent fishermen have ordinary nets, 8 per cent fishermen have nylon net while 9 per cent fishermen have traditional boats like catamaran and 8 per cenr fishermen are having mechanized or motorized boats such as BLCS, IBE and OBM engine boats. The sample fishermen who do not have any crafts and gears, they go on fishing on other boats as *raita* (Labour Contract).

Per Capita Expenditure of Non-defaulter Fishermen who have Obtained Institutional Finance in Ganjam District

The entire sample of 1200 fishermen, have obtained credit from different financial institutions such as commercial banks, co-operative banks, RRBs etc. Out of which only 510,842 have repaid their loan. The pattern of expenditure of non-defaulter fishermen is shown in Table 6.8 and Fig. 6.12 and 6.13.

Table 6.8. Per Capita Expenditure of Non-defaulter Fishermen in Ganjam District

(In hundred)

Sl. No.	Pattern of expenditure	Amount Rs.	%
1.	Food	1556	28
2.	Health	1021	18
3.	Education	947	17
4.	Maintenance	362	7
5.	Social customs	387	7
6.	Liquor	448	8
7.	Repair of boats and nets	426	8
8	Ornaments	37	1
9.	Payment of loan	347	6
	Total	5531	100

Source: Compiled from the Questionnaire.

The pie chart (Fig. 6.13) reveals the pattern of expenditure of different items. Twenty eight per cent fishermen expend on food, 18 per cent on health, 17 per cent on education, 7 per cent on maintenance 8 per cent

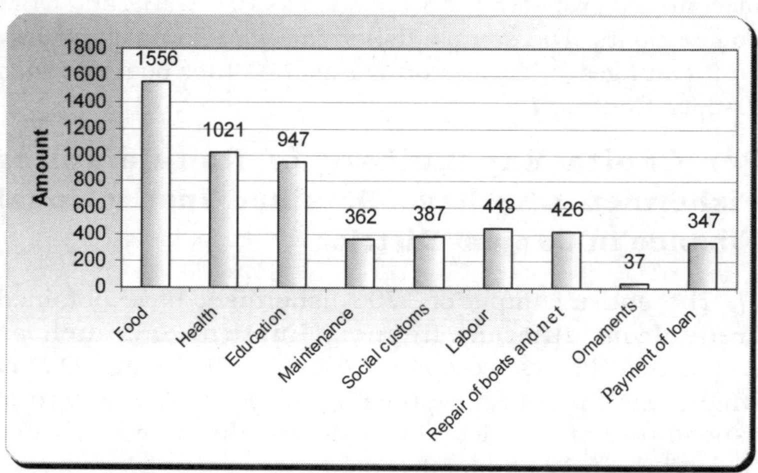

Fig. 6.12. Per Capita expenditure of Non-defaulter Fishermen in Ganjam District

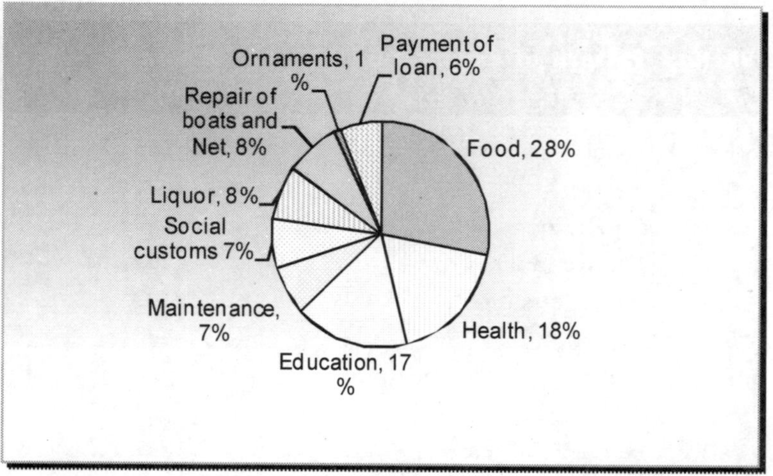

Fig. 6.13. Expenditure of Non-defaulter Fishermen in Ganjam District

on social custom, 8 per cent on liquor, 8 per cent on repair of boat and net, one per cent on ornaments and 6 per cent towards repayments of loan. It is observed that there is susbstantial amount of expenditure on liquor. Further, the respondents has made provision for repayment of loans.

Per Capita Expenditure of Fefaulter Fishermen who have Obtained Institutional Finance in Ganjam District

Out of 1200 fishermen who have obtained finance from different financial institutions, 690 fishermen constituting 58 are defaulters. The per Capita expenditure of defaulter fishermen is shown in Table 6.9 and Fig. 6.14 and Fig. 6.15.

Table 6.9. Per-Capita Expenditure of Defaulter Fishermen in Ganjam District

(Rs. hundred)

Sl. No.	Pattern of expenditure	Expenditure	% of expenditure
1.	Food	1,738	33
2.	Health	838	15
3.	Education	285	5
4.	Maintenance	290	5
5.	Social custom	297	5
6.	Liquor	1,280	23
7.	Repair of boat and Net	662	12
8.	Ornament	109	2
	Total	5499	100

Source: Compiled from the questionnaire

From the pie chart (Fig. 6.15) it is clear that top priority was given to food i.e. 33 per cent and the most neglected item was education constituting 5 per cent. Fifteen per cent of expenditure on health is made. A good deal of money is also spent on liquor constituting 23 per cent. The per cent is spent on ornaments, although it is very negligible. Five per cent expenditure on maintenance and 5 per cent spent on social custome. As education was not given priority. The result of which their conditions remain unchanged. Less importance was also given to health. They spent a lot of money 5 per cent on social customs such as marriage, birth, death etc. They participate in different religious functions.

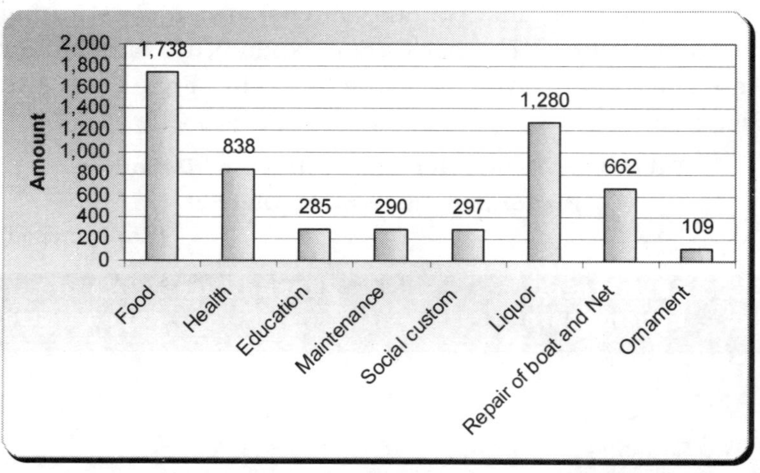

Fig. 6.14. Expenditure Ppattern No. of Fishermen in Ganjam District.

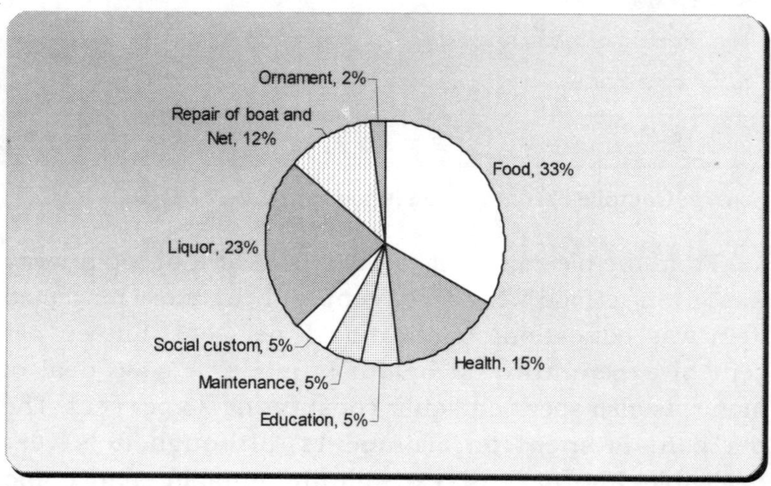

Fig. 6.15. Pattern of Expenditure of Defaulter Fishermen in Ganjam District.

Comparison between Per Capita Expenditure in Respect of Defaulter and Non-defaulter Fishermen of the District

Out of the 1200 fishermen, 510 (42%) fishermen have repaid the loan whereas 690 (68%) sample fishermen are defaulters. A comparison is made to find out the per capita expenditure of defaulter fishermen and non-defaulter fishermen and reason are depicted in Table 6.10.

Table 6.10. Comparison of Pattern of Expenditure between Defaulter and Non-defaulter Fishermen in Ganjam

(In hundred)

Sl. No.	Pattern of expenditure	Non-defaulter (Rs.)	Per cent (%)	Defaulter (Rs.)	Per cent (%)
1.	Food	1556	28	1738	33
2.	Health	1021	18	838	15
3.	Education	947	17	285	5
4.	Maintenance	362	7	290	5
5.	Social custom	387	7	297	5
6.	Liquor	448	8	1280	23
7.	Repair of Boat and net	426	8	662	12
8.	Ornament	37	1	109	2
9.	Repayment of loan	347	6	—	—
	Total	5,531	100.00	5,499	100

Source : Compiled from the questionnaire.

Table 6.10 reveals that the sample non-defaulter fishermen have spent on food 28 per cent, on health 18 per cent, on education 17 per cent, on maintenance 7 per cent, social customs 7 per cent, on liquor 8 per cent. on repair of boat and net 8 per cent, on ornaments one per cent and repayment of loan 6 per cent.

The sample defaulters have spent their money on food 33 per cent, on health 15 per cent, on education 5 per cent, on maintenance 5 per cent, on social customs 5 per cent, on liquor 23 per cent, on repair of boat and net 12 per cent, on ornaments 2 per cent.

On comparison it was found that the defaulter fishermen have spent Rs. 1280 (23%) towards consumption of liquor while the non-defaulter fishermen spent only Rs. 448 (8%) on liquor. Similarly defaulter fishermen spent Rs. 1738 (33%) on food while the non-defaulter have spent Rs. 1556 (28%) on food. The most important factor is that the non-defaulter fishermen made provision towards repayment of loan.

Economic Conditions of Fishermen who have Repaid the Loan

From the sample 1200 fishermen, only 510 (42%) repaid the loan. Economic condition of these fishermen, who have repaid their loan, is shown in Table 6.11 and Fig. 6.16 and 6.17.

Table 6.11. Economic conditions of fishermen who have repaid loan in Ganjam District

Sl. No.	Expenditure made by sample fishermen who have repaid loan	No. of sample fishermen	%
1.	Furniture	17	3
2.	TV set	24	5
3.	Radio	15	3
4.	Bicycles	37	7
5.	Small boats	187	37
6.	Net	131	26
7.	Small freezing box	32	6
8.	House (converting) thatched house into asbestos roof	15	3
9.	Education	52	10
	Total	510	100

Source : Compiled from the questionnaire.

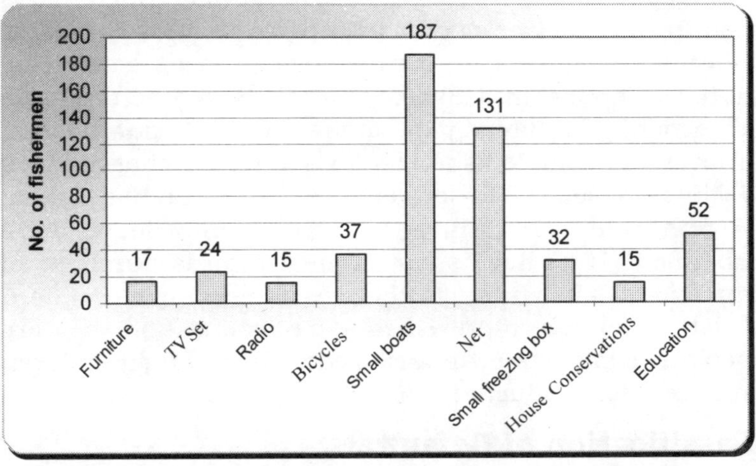

Fig. 6.16. Economic Conditions of Non-defaulter Fishermen in Ganjam District

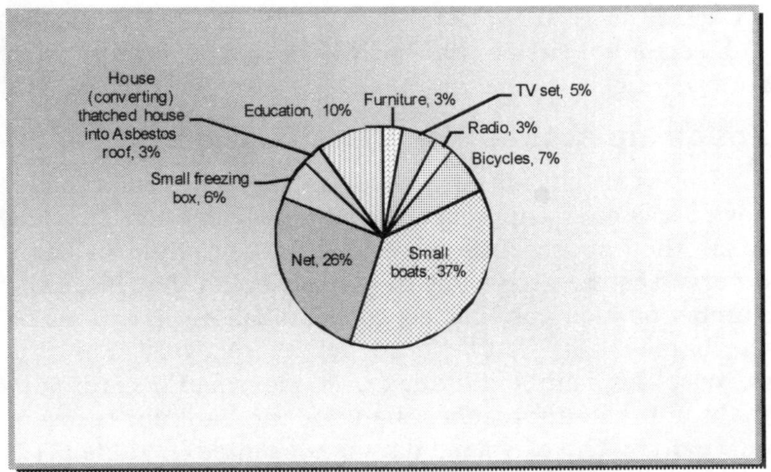

Fig. 6.17. Economic Condition of Non-defaulter Fishermen in Ganjam district in percentage.

Table 6.11 reveals that out of 1200 sample fishermen 510 (42%) have repaid the loan. After repayment 187 sample fishermen (37%) spent money on productive use like purchasing boat, 131 fishermen (26%) haves spent on purchasing of nets. Thirty-two sample fishermen (16%) spent their money on purchaser of small ice box, 15 sample fishermen (13%) have spent money towards converting thatched house into asbestos roof. Seventeen sample fishermen (3%) have spent money towards purchase of furniture 24 sample fishermen (5%) have purchased black & white TV set, 15 fishermen (3%) have purchase radio, 37 fishermen (7%) have purchased bicycle, and 52 fishermen (10%) have spent money towards purchase of educational kits. In short the overall economic standard of fishermen has improved to some extent, and they are spending some money towards, education of their children and use it for productive purpose.

Classification of Defaulters

The borrowers of the district Ganjam, who have not repaid their loan are referred to here as the defaulting borrowers. Out of the sample 1200 borrowers 510 (42.5%) are found to be defaulters. An attempt has been mode in this sector to classify the barrowers and defaulters from various angles.

Follow up Action wise Classification

The bank official for recovering the sanctioned loans, have occasionally approach the sample fishermen. In some cases they successfully recover the debt while in same other cases they have failed. It is observed that more the number of such approaches, called as follow up actions by the bank staff, better would be the recovery. For this purpose the sample data has been classified according to the number of approaches made by the bank for recovery of the dues. The classified data is presented in Table 6.12.

Table 6.12 reveals that out of the sample 1200 fishermen a sizeable number of fishermen 576 (65%), have not been approached by bank officials. Hundred seventy-nine sample fishermen (55 %) have been approached once by bank official, 71 sample fishermen (46%) were approached twice and 17 fishermen (47%) were approached more than thrice.

Table 6.12. Classification of Borrowers according to number of approaches by bank officials

(In Nos.)

Sl. No.	Named of the Subdivision/ NAC		Nil	Once	Twice	Thrice	More than thrice	Total
1.	Berhampur	B	123	105	72	49	6	355
		D	66	45	21	24	2	148
		%	54	43	29	48	33	42
2.	Bhanjanagar	B	93	82	25	18	5	223
		D	60	35	12	9	1	117
		%	65	42	48	50	20	52
3.	Chatrapur	B	216	81	27	19	14	357
		D	121	57	14	11	6	209
		%	56	70	52	58	43	59
4.	Gopalpur NAe	B	144	57	32	21	11	265
		D	128	42	24	14	8	216
		%	88	73	75	67	73	81
5.	Total	B	576	325	156	107	36	1200
		D	375	179	71	58	17	690
		%	65	55	46	54	47	58

B = Borrowers D = Defaulter % = percentage.
Source: Compiled from in Questionnaire.

Quantum of Credit wise Classification

In quantum of credit-wise classification usually it is very difficult to repay the credit if the size of the amount is high and is not difficult if it is less. This trouble has been found with this sample also. The borrowers and the defaulters are classified according to their quantum or magnitude of the loan amount. This classification has been presented in Table 6.13.

Table 6.13 reveals that highest number of borrowers 698 (58%) have secured loan which is less than Rs. 4,000. The number of defaulters in this category are 278 (40%). Similarly the loanee fishermen in the range of Rs. 4000 -

Rs. 9000 are 222 (19%), out of which 167 (75%) are defaulters. Number of defaulters are 127 (86%) in the range of Rs. 9,000 - Rs. 14,000, 79 defaulter fishermen (88%) are in the range of Rs. 14,000 - Rs. 19,000. Highest number of defaulter 39 fishermen (91%) have secured loan amount of more than Rs. 19,000. On observation it is found that when the loan amount is on rise the number of defaulter fishermen are also more. It means mathematically the quantum of loan and its repayment varies inversely.

Table 6.13. Size of Loan of Borrower/Defaulter in Ganjam District

(Rs. in thousand)

	Less than Rs. 4000	Rs. 4000- Rs. 9000	Rs. 9000- Rs. 14,000	Rs. 14,000-- Rs. 19,000	More than Rs. 19,000	Total (Rs.)
B.	698	222	147	90	43	1200
%	58	19	12	8	3	100
R	420	55	20	11	04	510
%	60	25	14	12	9	42
D	278	167	127	79	39	690
%	40	75	86	88	91	58

B= Borrowers % = percentage

On the Basis of Liquor Addicted Fishermen

Usually it is important to find out the impact of liquor on sample fishermen of the district. General belief is that drinking habit among fishermen leads to default in loan repayment. The drinking habit of sample fishermen are divided according to their age group. It is depicted in table 6.14.

From Table 6.14 it is quiet clear that drinking habit is the highest among the age group of 15-30 and also the number of defaulters is highest i.e. 447 totalling (78%) in this particular age group. The percentage of number of defaulters is lowest constituting 38 per cent in the age group of 30-45 and 45-60.

Table 6.14. Drinking Habit among Defaulter Sample Fishermen in Ganjam District

(In No.)

Sl. No.	Name of the Subdivisions/ NAC		Age Group 15-30	30-45	45-60	60 & More	Total
1.	Berhampur	B	176	117	38	24	355
		D	106	27	9	6	148
		%	60	23	24	25	42
2.	Bhanjanagar	B	94	78	36	15	223
		D	72	29	9	7	117
		%	76	37	25	47	52
3.	Chatrapur	B	171	118	33	35	357
		D	148	36	14	11	209
		%	86	31	42	31	59
4.	Gopalpur NAc	B	135	64	27	39	265
		D	121	52	19	24	216
		%	89	81	70	62	81
5.	Total	B	576	377	134	113	1200
		D	447	144	51	48	690
		%	78	38	38	42	58

B = Borrower D = Defaulter % = Percentage

Source: Compiled from the questionnaire.

Gopalpur NAC leads the number of defaulter with 89 percent in the age group of 15-30. This might be due to the reason that the younger ones are erratic and try to lead their life with fun and frolic.

Defaulter in Marine and Inland Sectors

Out of the 1200 sample fishermen 600 from marine sector have availed credit and equal number from inland sector have availed credit. The classification of defaulting fishermen of Ganjam district according to marine sector and inland sector is shown in Table 6.15.

Table 6.15. Classification of sample Fishermen and Defaulters in Marine and Inland sector in Ganjam District

(In No.)

Sl. No.	Subdivisions /NAC		Marine	Inland	Total
1.	Berhampur	B	157	198	355
		D	54	94	148
		%	34	47	42
2.	Bhanjanagar	B	—	223	223
		D	—	117	117
		%	—	52	52
3.	Chatrapur	B	198	159	357
		D	151	58	209
		%	76	36	59
4.	Gopalpur NAC	B	245	20	26'5
		D	203	13	216
		%	82	65	81
5.	Total	B	600	600	1,200
		D	408	282	690
		%	68	47	58

B = Borrower D = Defaulter % = Percentage

Source: Compiled from the questionnaire.

Table 6.15 reveals that the number of fishermen in marine and inland sector as 600 each. The defaulter represent 68 per cent in marine sector and 47 per cent in Inalnd sector. The comparison reveals that in marine sector the number of defaulter are 282, which is higher than defaulter of inland sector. The percentage of defaulters in marine sector in Gopalpur is highest (82%) in and lowest in Berhampur Subdivision (34%). Bhanjanagar Subdivision is not included in marine sector. In inland sector highest number of defaulters (65%) belongs to Gopalpur and the lowest i.e., 36% belongs to Chatrapur.

Time Lagwise Classification

It is observed that the bank officials need some time for sanctioning the loan proposal of the sample borrowers. This period is known as processing time. This processing time for the sample borrowers varies from 2 to 65 days for scrutinsing and sanctioning the loan proposal to the prospective applicants. A time gap is created from the date of applying for a loan and getting the loan by the borrower. This gap is termed as 'timelag'. The sample borrowers have been classified according to the time lag in sanctioning of loans by the banks, which is shown in table 6.16.

Table 6.16. Classification of Fishermen According to Ttime Lag

(In days)

Sl. No.	Name of the Subdivisions/ NAC		Age Group				
			0-15	15-30	30-60	60 and More	Total
1.	Berhampur	B	54	103	74	124	355
		D	13	21	24	90	148
		%	24	20	32	73	42
2.	Bhanjanagar	B	24	37	71	91	223
		D	5	18	17	77	117
		%	21	49	24	85	52
3.	Chatrapur	B	57	32	86	182	357
		D	6	4	38	161	209
		%	11	13	44	88	59
4.	Gopalpur NAe	B	20	40	97	108	265
		D	7	36	75	98	216
		%	35	90	77	91	81
5.	Total	B	155	212	328	505	1200
		D	31	79	154	426	690
		%	20	37	47	84	58

B = Borrowers D = Defaulters % = Percentage

Source: Compiled from the questionnaire.

Table 6.16 reveals that out of 1200 sample fishermen, 505 fishermen (42%) had to wait for more than 60 days. 328 borrowers (27%) had to wait for 30 to 60 days, 212 fishermen (18%) had to wait for 15 to 30 days and the remaining 153 borrowers (14%) are lucky enough to get their credit within a fortnight. The overall percentage of defaulter is 58 where as their percentage is 84 when the time lag includes 60 and more 37 per cent where the time lag is 15-30 days, 47 per cent where as the time lag ranges from 30 to 60 days and 20 per cent where as the time lag ranges from 0-15 days. Thus it is clear that the percentage of defaulting fishermen is increasing with more time lag. It may be due to the reason that borrower had to run to the bank for sanction of loan which makes them lose their daily wages. After the sanction of loan the time of need might have expired. As a consequence they might have utilized the loan for some other purpose of urgency of that time like repayment of other loans which became due.

Chronic and Non-chronic Defaulters

The sample fishermen of the sample district are classified according to the period of tune passed since the credit has become due for repayment. There is no definition available regarding the meaning of chronic defaulters it is presumed that the borrowers who are defaulters for more than five years are chronic defaulters and the rest are non-chronic. The classification of the borrowers and the defaulters in various subdivisions and Gopalpur NAC of Ganjam district is depicted in Table 6.17.:

Table 6.17 reveals that out of the total defaulters (690) 475 are chronic (68.84%) while the rest 215 are non-chronic defaulter (31.16%). The comparison shows that out of the 475 chronic defaulters as high as 183 (39%) belongs to Gopalpur NAC. The least number of 74 chronic defaulters (16%) belongs to Chatrapur Similarly out of 690 sample defaulters, 215 (31.16 %) are non-chronic. Out of 215 non-chronic defaulters, maximum 155 (62.79%) belong to Chatrapur. While the minimum number of 21 (17.95%) non-chronic defaulters belongs to Bhanjanagar.

Table 6.17. Classification of Defaulters on the Basis of Chronic and Non-chronic in Ganjam District

(In No.)

Sl. No.	Name of the Sub Division/NAC		Chronic	Non-Chronic	Total
		D	122	26	148
1.	Berhampur	P	82.43	17.57	100
		D	76	21	117
2.	Bhanjanagar	P	82.05	17.95	100
		D	74	135	209
3.	Chatrapur	P	135.41	64.59	100
		D	183	33	216
4.	Gopalpur	P	84.72	15.28	100
	Total	D	475	215	690
		P	68.84	31.16	100

D = Defaulters P = Percentage.

Source : Compiled from the questionnaire

Caste-wise Classification

Classification on the basis of the caste of sample fishermen and defaulters is depicted in the table 6.18.

The figures Table 6.18 makes it clear that out of 1200 sample fishermen 130 (11%) are SC, 164 (14%) are ST, 529 (72%) are OBC and 377 (37%) are of general castes. The percentage of defaulters to the total sample is 58 where as it is 72 per cent among OBC, whereas it is 56 per cent in case of S.C., 59 per cent in respect of ST and 37 per cent among general caste borrowers. Comparison of defaulter sample fishermen reveals that among OBC caste borrowers, the defaulters percentage ranges from 61 to 90 per cent. Whereas among SC it ranges from 41 to 70 per cent, and among STs it ranges from 47 to 73 per cent. The defaulters are low in general castes which ranges from 26 to 55 per cent. The high percentage of defaulters belongs to OBC caste, perhaps the reason is that OBC caste mainly consists of Noliyaes whose economic standard is very poor.

Table 6.18 Caste-wise Defaulter Fishermen in Ganjam District

(In nos)

Sl. No.	Name of the Subdivisions/ NAC		SC	ST	OBC	General	Total
1.	Berhampur	B	39	51	109	156	355
		D	16	24	67	41	148
		%	41	47	61	26	42
2.	Bhanjanagar	B	21	29	58	115	223
		D	12	16	36	53	117
		%	57	55	62	46	52
3.	Chatrapur	B	29	46	185	97	357
		D	16	34	120	39	209
		%	55	73	65	40	59
4.	Gopalpur NAC	B	41	38	177	09	265
		D	29	22	160	05	216
		%	70	57	90	55	81
5.	Total	B	130	164	529	377	1200
		D	73	96	383	138	690
		%	56	59	72	37	58

B = Borrower D = Defaulter % = Percentage

Source : Complied from the questionnaire

Literacy-wise Classification

The sample fishermen are classified according to their literacy standards into four groups namely. (*a*) illiterates, (*b*) under 10th standard, (*c*) under graduate and (*d*) graduates and above. The classifications of the borrowers and the defaulters fishermen in the district according to their literacy standard is reflected in Table 6.19.

Table 6.19 reveals that out of 690 defaulters of sample fishermen 624 (61%) are illiterate and the rate of defaulting borrower fishermen is high among illiterate followed by below 10th standard 46 (33%). The rate of defaulters among illiterates varies from 45 per cent to 87 per cent. The least number of defaulter is 5 (21%) among graduates and post-graduates. The reason may be that the literates are well-aware of the rules and regulations of bank lending, and by repaying the loan, they can avail the amount of subsidy and can hope to get further financial help from the banks in future. This advantage is not known to the among illeterate and less educated borrowers. Ignorance of law is a fact which is applicable to illiterates.

Table 6.19. Classification of Sample Fishermen's Defaulter Fishermen According to their Literacy Standard

(In No.)

Sl. No.	Name of the Subdivisions/ NAC		SC	ST	OBC	General	Total
1.	Berhampur	B	265	56	26	8	355
		D	133	7	7	1	148
		%	45	13	27	12.5	42
2.	Bhanjanagar	B	189	20	8	6	223
		D	101	11	3	2	117
		%	53	55	38	33	52
3.	Chatrapur	B	305	39	7	6	357
		D	189	15	3	2	209
		%	62	38	43	133	59
4.	Gopalpur NAC	B	231	24	6	4	265
		D	201	13	2	—	216
		%	87	54	33	—	81
5.	Total	B	990	139	47	24	1200
		D	624	46	15	5	690
		%	61	33	32	121	

B= Borrowers D= Defaulters

Source: Compiled from the questionnaire

Age-wise Classification

The age of sample fishermen ranges from 18 years to 60 years. So for convenience all the sample borrowers have been classified into three age groups viz. (*i*) 18 to 30 years, (*ii*) 30 to 45 years, and (*iii*) 45 to 60 years. The borrowers and the defaulters, according to this classifications are shown in Table 6.20.

Table 6.20. Age-wise classification of defaulter Fishermen in Ganjam district

(In No)

Sl. No.	Name of Sub divisions/ NAC		Age group 18-30	30-45	45-60	Total
1.	Berhampur	B	224	79	52	355
		D	90	42	16	148
		%	40	53	31	42
2.	Bhanjanagar	B	154	47	22	223
		D	67	31	19	117
		%	44	66	86	52
3.	Chatrapur	B	248	71	38	357
		D	121	56	32	209
		%	49	79	84	59
4.	Gopalpur NAC	B	201	41	23	265
		D	157	38	21	216
		%	78	92	91	81
	Total	B	827	238	135	1200
		D	435	167	88	690
		%	53	70	65	58

B= Borrower D= Defaulter

Source : Compiled from the questionnaires

Table 6.20 reveals that at the district level 690 (58%) sample fishermen are defaulters. Among them the defaulters of the age group 30-45 is with 167 (70%), followed by the defaulters in the age group of 45-60 with 88 (65%). The defaulters are less in the age group of 18-30 with 53 per cent defaulters (435). The reason may be that the younger age group is working hard to utilise their fund in a proper way and are very particular about repaying the loan in right time as far as practicable. The middle age group (30-45) are loaded with financial problems, family responsibilities and they perhaps utilize the loan in non-productive purposes. Hence the percentage of defaulter is high in this particular group:

Chapter 7 Findings and Suggestions

Introduction

As the concluding chapter of the study, this chapter highlights the summary of some major findings of the study. In this chapter an attempt has been made to put the formulated hypotheses to test and draw inferences basing on the findings. Few suggestions also follow basing on the inferences. In fact, the practical utility of the present study is examined, followed by a list of key and important issues for further study on the subject.

Summary of the Major Findings (Chapterwise)

Socio-economy Profile of Fishermen in India and Orissa

From pre-historic period fishes have been used as protein rich diet by human beings, India is the seventh largest fish producer in the world covering an area of 3.29 million square km. Fishing is broadly classified into inland fisheries and marine fisheries. Inland fisheries cover rivers, mangroves, estuaries, backwater, lagoon etc. India occupies second position in inland fish production of the world. Marine fishery is wholly a capture-oriented sector. India has a coastline of 8085 km having 3,638 fishing villages. India occupies tenth position in total fish production of the world. Marine fishery resources are broadly divided into two types: Demersal and Pelagic. In India there are twelve bio-geographiczones. Inland capture fishery contributes at least 30 per cent of the total fish production.

Marine fishery helps to earn foreign exchange for the country. There is a steady increase of foreign exchange. In the year 2004-05 India earned Rs. 7245.30 crores by exporting fish to other countries. The chief importing countries are Japan, U.S.A., European Union, China, India also exports marine products to these countries. The ports used for export of marine products are Chennai, Kochi, Kolkata, etc.

The State of Orissa, popularly known as "Odisha" is situated in the eastern coast of Indian peninsula. The State comprises of 3 revenue divisions, 30 districts, 58 sub-divisions, 171 Tahasils, 314 blocks, 6234 gram panchayats and 51,349 villages. The population of the State is 368 lakhs as per 2001 census. 35.8 per cent of the State's population is cultivator. The per capita income is Rs. 6,555. In 2004-05 per capita availability of land comes to 0.15 hectare. The irrigation potential of the State from all sources are 26.96 lakh hectare. The total livestock population of the state is 240.22 lakh. It is headed by cattle population of 142.8 lakh. The total forest area of the State is 58,136 sq km. The literacy rate has increased to 63.8 per cent, but the State has poor transport and communication systems. Paradeep is the only port through which export from the State takes place. The State has vast mineral resources, chief among these is chromite. Health system of the State includes 174 hospitals, 231 community health centres, 120 primary health centres. The State has 362 large and medium industries with an investment of Rs. 3600.21 crore. There are also 4511 small industries. Different poverty allevtion scheme has also been introduced by the State government. The State has great potential for both marine and inland fisheries. The State has a coastline of 480 km, 6,70,017 hectare of water area and 4,17,537 hectare of brackish water area. The total inland fishermen population is 6,82,378 and marine fishermen population is 3,32,792.

Fish production of Orissa, mounted to 315.80 tmt in 2004-05 registering an increase of 2.88 per cent, Disposition of fish also increasesed from 26.120 tmt in 1999-2000 to 315.80 tmt in 2004-05. Fresh water fish product of Ganjam is 17.81 tmt during 2004-05. A Centrally- sponsored scheme called "Fish Farmers Development Agency" is being implemented to develop such areas and to provide technical assistance to fish farmers. A total 30 FFDAs are functioning in the State. Similary to improve pisciculture in brackish water area FFDA has been set up but there is a decrease in production in brackish water from 24,447 mt in 2003-04 to 23,776 mt in 2004-05. This happens due to fall in production in Chilika lake. In Chilika the production of fish was 13,098 mt for which 162 crafts were operated. The per capita annual consumption fish has increased from 8.28 kg in 2003-04 to 8.35 kg in 2004-05. The fresh water fish production from different sources comes to 170.09 mt. In the year 2004-05 to produce quality fish seed, 19 departmental hatcheries, 5 hatcheries of OPDC and 22 hatcheries in private sector have been set up.

Marine fisheries play an important role in earning foreign exchange. Marine fish production of the State has increased by 9.82 per cent in the year 2004-05. Marine products of Orissa is exported to foreign countries such as Japan, China, U.S.A., U.K. etc. In the year 2005-06 the total estimate of fish was 86.799 mt. But 37.01 tint of freshwater fish was imported by the State. In the State different fishermen welfare schemes have implemented. The Government has set up 977 primary fishermen co-operative societies in the State. The contribution of Orissa in fish production is increasing from 39 per cent during the year 1995-96 to 47 per cent during the year 2004-05. Similarly fish production has also increased from 1,00,036 tmt in 1995-96 to 1,47,416 tmt in 2004-05.

Socio-economic Condition of Fishermen of Sample District

The name 'Ganjam' has its origin from the word "Ganj-i-am', which in Persian language word means the 'Granary of the world'. The district is bounded by Boudh-Kandhamal district in north, Srikakulam district of Andhra Pradesh and Gajapati district of Orissa in the South, Bay of Bengal and Puri district in the East. The total area of the district is 8206 square kilometres. It has three Sub-divisions, 22 Blocks, 3212 villages, 14 Tahasils, 17 Notified Area Councils, 475 Gram Panchayats, 28 Police Stations, 12 Fire Stations and 12 Assembly Constituencies. The district receive an annual rainfall covering only 129.56 cm. The trend of production is not satisfactory. 'Rushikulya Irrigation System' is the only major project of the district. The district is covered with homogeneous temperature throughout the year. The total population of the district was 31.37 lakhs as per 2001 census. It as 8.45 per cent of total population and occupied first in population in the State. The literacy rate of the district was 62.94 per cent.

About 63.14 per cent of total workforce constituted cultivators and agricultural labourers. Unemployment was the major problem for the development of the district. Co-operative sector plays an important role in providing finance for both agricultural and non-agricultrual sectors throughout the year. Agricultural loan has increased to Rs. 1,559.11 lakh. Rice is the main crop with a total production of 58,11,184 quantals in 2004-05 followed by sugar. Irrigation is provided to 30,458 ha. Consumption of fertilizers was also increased to 30,650 mt in the year 2003-04. The district has an efficient transport system, the length of State highway is 67.3 km., but there is no express highway in the district. But the industrial scenario is not encouraging. The district had only 3 medium industries and 313 small scale industries providing a limited (1377) employment opportunity. Daily and weekly markets are found in Berhampur, Hinjilicut, Aska, Bhanjanagar, Kabisuryanagar, Bellaguntha, Buguda, Kodala. Huma is the largest dry fish market in Asia. The export products of the district are *pattasaree*, silver product, dry fish and tobacco. There is development in general as well as technical education in the district. The district had 2936 primary schools, 642 middle schools, 43 secondary' schools, and 43 colleges dureing study period. The general health system is also found satisfactory.

The district had 1541 beds in Allopathic hospitals, 25 beds at Homoeopathic hospitals, and 25 beds at Ayurvedic hospitals. The district had 227 branches of 26 banks which includes 65 branches of Regional Rural banks, and 124 branches of commercial banks. Life Insurance Company had set-up six branches in the district.

The district has potential for both inland and marine fisheries. It has a coastline of 60 kilometres with 28 marine fishing villages with a population of 37,506. The marine fishing is dominated by Noliya, Kandra, Sondi, Keuta and Kanatia communities. For fishing in the sea they use different types of traditional crafts and gears. These communities are basically living near the sea-shore. The district has infrastructure facilities which included 16 fish landing centres, three fishery jetties, one fishing harbour at Gopalpur and one fish landing platform.

The district is considered to be rich in aquacultural resources in the form of fresh water and brackish water. The district's inland population was 93,686 living in 444 fishermen villages. The total water spread area was 485.90 hectares and water utilized area is 3180.06 hectare. There were 5 departmental farms in the district. There was also an increase in spawn and fry production. For the development of inland fishing FFDA was established in the year 1976. Similarly the Government has formulated 'State Reservoir Fishery Policy'. Fisheries Department had transferred their reservoirs to PMFC's and SHG groups. Finance was provided through commercial banks and co-operatives.

Role of Different Banks in Financing Fishermen

Commercial banks played important role towards the development of trade, commerce, agriculture and industry of the country. They accept deposits from the public and grant loans to the pubic. They also deal with different negotiable instruments like cheque, bills of exchange promissory note etc. India has a large network of banking system. Fourteen banks were nationalized in the year 1969 and six more banks were nationalized in the year 1980. In Ganjam there are 26 commercial banks having 226 branch during study period. Regional Rural Banks also play an important role. The mobilization of deposits by commercial banks and RRBs have increased by 15 per cent and 5 per cent respectively during 2005-06. Commercial banks played an important role towards development of fishery sector of Ganjam district. Apex level organizations like NABARD, NCDC, FFDAs provide finance to banks which in turn refinance to fishermen. Finance made to the FFDAs was Rs. 28,979 lakhs during 2003-04, Rs. 54,500 lakhs in 2004-05 and Rs. 99.26 lakhs during 2005-06. Commercial banks also provide finance to pond development programme. Co-operatives also play an important role towards the development of marine fishermen. They have provided 32 beach landing craft through NCDC programmes. They have provided finance towards motorisation of traditional crafts. A new policy was introduced in the inland sector which is known as 'State Reservoir Policy'. A total of Rs. 10,00,620 is spent towards renovations of reservoirs and MIPs under this policy.

NABARD has played an important role by providing finance towards renovation of tanks, reservoirs, fisheries, motorised boats etc. In the year 2003-04, NABARD had financed Rs.146.94 lakhs, in 2004-05 it had increased to Rs. 282.07 lakhs and in the year 2005-06 it was decreased to Rs. 222.30 lakhs.

Russhikulya Gramya Bank, the Regional Rural Bank of the district have financed through its 66 branches. CARD Bank, B.C.C.B banks as well as Aska Co-operative Central Bank have also financed to fishermen society in the district.

In order to improve socio-economic condition of the

fishermen of the district different schemes were implemented which includes IRDP scheme, Bay of Bengal Programme, K.C.C. and STEP etc.

Supply and Demand of Fund according to the Need of the Fishermen

According to the need of the fishermen for the purpose of studying the demand, the supply and the credit gap of fund sample of 600 from marine sector and 600 from inland sector were taken into account in the sample district of Ganjam which are selected at random. The sample district Ganjam was divided into 3 subdivisions, Berhampur, Chatrapur, Bhanjanagar and one Notified Area Council (Gopalpur).

It is observed that all the 1200 sample fishermen of the district were not supplied with the full credit amount. Out of the sample fishermen, 690 are defaulters, who account for 58 per cent. Among the defaulters 408 belong to marine sector and 282 belong to inland sector.

Borrowers on the basis of sex revealrs that male borrowers are 1038 (87%) and female defaulters are 162 (13%) only. Borrowers on the basis of literacy revealed that number of illeterate borrowers were 990 (82.5%) and literacy borrowers are 210 (17.5%).

Similarly in Inland sector out of 600 sample fishermen 282 are defaulters totaling 47 per cent, while number of defaulters in marine sector are 408 constituting 68 per cent. Out of 600 sample on a whole the fishery sector of Ganjam district shows that number of defaulters are 690 which is 58 per cent. The total demand for fund is Rs. 43,61,363 and total supply of fund is Rs. 32,82386 and the credit-gap is Rs. 10,78.977.

Non-institutional agencies play a important role by providing finance to meet the credit gap of fishermen in the district. Non-institutional agency includes *sahukars*, landlords, friends, relatives, neighbours and others. The total demand for fund is Rs. 8,01,312 and the total supply of fund is Rs. 7,92,503 and hence the gap is only Rs. 8,809.

This means non-institutional agency supplies 99 per cent of the total amount demanded by the fishermen of the district. This is because of the liberal attitude by the non-institutional agency towards fishermen of the district.

Socio-economic Condition of Fishermen—An Analysis

This chapter deals with various reasons responsible for socio-economic conditions of sample fishermen in Ganjam district. The sample district is divided into two sectors such as marine and inland sector. A sample of 1,200 fishermen were taken with 600 from marine and 600 from inland sector. The sample district consists of Berhampur, Chatrapur, Bhanjanagar subdivision and one NAC such as Gopalpur.

Development of a country depends very much on its availability of infrastructure facilities which consist of fishing jetties, harbours, cold storage, marketing and finance.

Forty per cent respondents complained that due to non-availability of sufficient fianance they are not in a position to purchase the essential articles for fishing. Nineteen per cent are of the view that lack of crafts and gears turned out to be a great obstacle for fishing.

Of late, sea fishing is not a regular business for fishermen. They go on fishing for only 169 days in a year. Forty two per cent fishermen are of the view that due to non-availability of modern fishing equipments like motorized boats, trawlers etc., they are not able to enter the deep sea which ultimately affects their catch. Eighteen per cent said that due to rough sea, bad weather conditions, cyclones etc their catch has been adversely affected Other causes are invasion of coastal area by Andhra trawlers, missile test conducted by army units at Gopalpur, medical problem etc. have also played an important role for the poor economic condition of the fishermen.

Poor marketing stands as an obstacle in the economic development of fishermen. Important reasons for poor marketing are lack of storage facility, lack of finance, transportation, interference by middlemens etc. Twenty per cent sample fishermen viewed that the interference by middlemen, brokers have forced them to sell their catch at a low price. Due to lack of storage facility near sea, and market places, the poor fishermen have no option but to sell their produce at a very low price.

Bank plays an important role in providing finance but in fishing sector it is observed that the fishermen are not interested to take money from the banks. Due to various reasons like negative attitude of the bank officials, policyies of the bank have discouraged them to take finance and opt for non-institutional finance.

The failure of commercial banks and cooperatives in providing loans to the needy fishermen has allowed the Regional Rural Bank (Rushikulya Gramya Bank) in Ganjam district to provide finance to rural massess through its 64 branches operating in the district. They provide finance for the purchase offish seeds, renovation of tanks, marketing, purchasing of crafts and gears etc. It provides finance to 493 fishermen totalling 47 per cent to a time of Rs. 15,07,439 and the number of defaulters are 34 per cent.

Due to their poor economic condition the fishermen are not able to purchase latest fishing equipments and have to be satisfied with their traditional crafts and gear while 72 per cent fishermen have no boats, only 9 per cent have traditional boats and 11 per cent have gears only.

The per capita expenditure of non-defaulter fishermen shows that they have spent 28 per cent on liquor, 18 per cent on health and 17 per cent on education. They spent only 8 per cent towards consumption of liquor and made provision of 6 per cent towards payment of loan.

Similarly the per capita expenditure of defaulter fishermen shows that they have spent 33 per cent on food, 15 per cent on health. But they spent only 5 per cent on education and a huge amount, i.e., 23 per cent an consumption of liquor. This makes them defaulters. They spent money towards unproductive purposes.

Distinction between factor of expenditure of defaulter and non-defaulter fishermen reveales that the non-defaulters have spent money in a productive purpose and they spent less on liquor. More importantly they have made a provision towards repayment of loan. The economic conditions of fishermen after repayment of loan showed that they have spent 26 per cent of their income on net; 37 per cent of their income on purchasing of boat; 10 per cent of their income on the education of their children.

Out of 1,200 sample borrowers, 690 (58 %) are found to be defaulters. Classification of defaulters on the basis of follow up action reveals that the bank officials have approached the sample fishermen occasionally.

Credit-wise classification reveals that when the amount of loan is higher, the number of defaultrs are also higher. Number of defaulters are 91 per cent when the amount of loan is more then 19,000. Similarly number of defaulters are less constituting 40 per cent when the loan amount is less than Rs. 4,000. Defaulters on the basis of liquor habit shows that the drinking habit is the highest in the age group of 15-30 and the number of defaulters is also the highest in this particular age group. Gopalpur NAC heads the number of defaulters with 89 per cent.

Number of defaulters in the fishery sector shows 408 defaulters i.e. per cent in marine sector and 282 (47%) in inland sector.

Defaulters on the basis of time lag shows that 505 fishermen (84%) have to wait for more than 60 days and 328 borrowers (47%) have to wait for 30 to 60 days. Hence, it is clear that percentage of defaulting borrower is increasing with more time lag and *vice versa.*

Defaulters on the basis of chronic and non-chronic divisions reveal that the borrowers who are defaulters for more than five years are chronic defaulters. It reveals that out of total defaulters of (690) 475 (68.84%) are chronic defaulters and 215 (31.16%) are non Chronic defaulters.

Classification of defaulters on the basis of casts reveals

that highest number of defaulters are OBC caste totalling 72 per cent, followed by S.Ts. constituting 59 per cent, S.Cs. 56 per cent and general castes constituting 37 per cent.

Classification of defaulters on the basis of literacy reveals that the highest number of defaulters are illiterate constituting 61 per cent; 33 per cent are below 10th standard; 32 per cent defaulters are undergraduates and 20 per cent defaulters are graduates and above.

Defaulter fishermen on the basis of age showed that 70 per cent are in the age group of 30-45, whereas the lowest number of defaulter totalling 53 per cent are in the age group of 18-30.

Testing of Hypotheses

In the light of the above findings the analysis made in the sixth chapter and the hypotheses formulated in the first chapter are tested here.

The RRB's are taking Very Important Steps in Financing the Fishermen of the District in Comparison to other Banks such as Commercial Banks and Cooperatives

The RRB's of the district are taking important steps to provide finance to the fishermen of the district with other banks such as commercial banks and co-operatives. The Regional Rural Bank's (RRB's) of the district are is named as Rushikulya Gramya Bank. The branches of the bank are located in the rural areas of the district and provide finance to the rural people to uplift their living standard. Table 6.6 reflects that RRB, itself had financed Rs. 15.07,439 to the fishermen of the district which contributes 47 per cent of the total finance, whereas the commercial banks provide finance of Rs. 14,88,895 to the sample beneficiaries which comes to 45 per cent of the total finance. The co-operative banks contribute 8 per cent of the total finance which comes to Rs. 2,86,117. Thus the hypothesis taken in the first chapter is proved to be correct and effective and hence the hypothesis is positive.

Non-marketing of Fish in Time Creates Problem For the Economic Development of Fishermen

Marketing is an important activity in any business. Brisk marketing means good economic condition of the sellers, but this aspect of life is quite absent in the sample population. This is reflected in Table 6.3. From the analysis of the table, it is observed that out of the twelve hundred beneficiacihis, all are not able to market the fish in time due to lack of transport facilities. Cold storage and the interference of the middlemen. These three account for 38 per cent. This shows that the marketing of raw fish is quite difficult for the fishermen. So the hypothesis taken here is not proved positive and hence not accepted.

The Fishermen are not using Modern Techniques for Catching Fish and they use Mostly Traditional Methods, which Create Restriction for the Economic Development of the Fishermen

Out of 1200 sample fishermen of Ganjam district, only 96 fishermen (8%) used motorized boat, 91 fishermen (8%) used nylon net for the purpose of fishing in the deep sea as reflected in Table 6.7. This means that 1013 fishermen are not able to use modern techniques for the purpose of fishing which accounts for their poor economic condition. So the hypothesis taken here is proved positive and correct.

Non-institutional Agencies play an Important Role in Financing the Fishermen in Comparision to the Institutional Agencies

The non-institutional agencies of the sample district play an important role in financing the fishermen of the district. The non-institutional agencies meet nearly 98.90 per cent as shown in Table 5.8 of the total demand of the fishermen of the sample district. Institutional agencies are able to meet 75.26 per cent of the total demand for the fishermen. However, in case of institutional finance

Rs. 43,61,363 were demanded by the fishermen of the sample district whereas all banks supplied only Rs. 32,82,386 to meet their credit needs as shown in Table 5.6. Thus all institutional financing agencies could meet only 75.26 per cent of their demand. So the hypothesis taken here is positive and proved to be 100 per cent correct.

The Borrowers who take more Loans from the Institutional Agencies, Repaid the same within a Specified Time, but the Number of Defaulters keep on Rising as the Loan Amount Decreases

Out of the sample borrowers of 1200, 690 sample borrower fishermen (58%) are found to be defaulters and 510 beneficiaries (42%) repay the loan in time. Further, in case of borrowers availing loan of more than Rs. 19,000 as shown in Table 6.13, the percentage of defaulters is 91 per cent. Furthermore, in case of beneficiaries availing less than Rs. 4,000 loan, the percentage of defaulters is 40 per cent. The number of defaulters rise as the loan of the borrower increases. Moreover, the percentage of defaulters is 91 per cent among borrowers availing loan of more than Rs. 19,000. So the borrowers availing more loan fail to repay in time and hence the defaulter percentage is higher in comparision to borrowers who are sanctioned less amount of loan. Thus the hypothesis taken here is proved wrong and incorrect.

As Sea Fishing is Seasonal, and Fish is not available Throughout the Year, it hampers the Economic Development of the Fishermen of the Sample District

Fishermen are very hardworking people. Given favourable conditions they would have never lagged behind in catching fish and getting a substantial profit. But these conditions are not found when the sample fishermen are asked about their low economic standard. They replied that they had always been at the mercy of weather conditions. Regarding their fishing activities, they are not engaged in this work for the reasons shown in Table 6.2 The table also shows that they are engaged only for 169 days in a year. Hence the hypothesis taken here is found to be correct and positive.

Suggestions

The financing institutions, government and other related parties are not taking proper steps to improve the socio economic conditions of fishermen. Steps have to be taken to tackle the situation efficiently depending upon the circumstances of the case. A few suggestions are put-forth hereunder to contain the situation properly:

1. There should be a strong fishermen association which will highlight their problems and hardships and offer solution to their problems.
2. Role of middlemen should be curtailed and thereby enabling the fishermen to sale their catch at better price to the ultimate consumer and receive a handsome profit.
3. Awareness programme should be undertaken by the government, NGO's and other institutions to discourage the fishermen from alcoholism and take steps for its eradication.
4. Indira Awas Yojana (IAY) should be provided to BPL group. The BPL group should be enlisted under the IAY for getting free shelter. The quota for BPL should increase.
5. Proper engagement, job facility for this community should be provided during off hours, which will enhance their income and enrich their living conditions.
6. Fisherwomen of the district should make different types of organisations such as Mahila Samitis, Co-operative societies which will help them to earn more for a decent living.
7. Fishermen should be aware of birth control, family planning, use of contraceptives, and other methods

so that they can have a small family for better living.

8. Fishermen should be well aware about the diseases such as polio, Hepatities-B, AID's, TB, Jaundice and other water-born diseases etc., their prevention, treatment and control. Hence, different health-oriented programmes should be implemented.
9. Different Self-Help Groups (SHGs), NGOs should come forward to help the economically handicapped and socially insolvent needy men to provide them two square meals, a piece of cloth, a small house to dwell in and clean water for drinking.
10. Steps should be taken to preserve their culture, heritage, social structure etc. Steps should be taken to reform them by organizing different cultural meets like, *Bela Mohatsav* etc. Recreational facilities like children parks should be provided to the children of the fishermen.
11. Proper education facilities should be provided to these people by opening schools, making provisions for night schools, providing educational kits to fishermen so that they can read and write and make a better living.
12. Adequate compensation package should be paid to the fishermen in Gopalpur because during the time of missile tests conducted by Army unit, they are prevented from entering into the sea.
13. Andhra Trawlers should not be allowed to enter the coastal area. Coast guards should be positioned to stop their entry.
14. The fishermen should be encouraged to use modern fishing equipments for deep sea fishing which will increase their income.
15. The infrastructure facilities like Jetty, cemented pucca base, roofed big house for keeping and weighing of fishes with proper weighing machine,

icing facilities, cold storage facilities should be provided.

16. Extension network of the fishery department should be strengthened for field demonstration, passing on the technical know how regarding seed, fertilizers etc. to the farmers.
17. The fish seeds should be made available to the farmers from the hatcheries in time.
18. The fish landing base should be connected with good road communication and must have basic infrastructure facilities like platform, electricity, drinking water facilities, diesel outlet etc.
19. Processing plants should be encouraged in private sector.
20. Fish farmers should be motivated for rearing of fingerlings/yearlings for stocking in water bodies for increasing rate of fish production.
21. Bank and other Non-financial Institutions should try to create saving habits among these people. Sanction of loan should be provided to them with less interest. A proper backup programme relating to utilization of loans should be conducted. Technical knowledge relating to pisciculture should be provided. Bankers have to show keen interest for financing pisciculture activities and establishment of process or storage units.
22. Steps should be taken by the Government NGOs to provide information about different policies framed by the Government and different development schemes so that the fishermen can avail the opportunities.

Practical Utility of the Study

The present study has highlighted the contribution of financial institutions towards socio-economic development of fishermen in Ganjam district. The finding of the study may prove to be useful to the planners of the State, to banks and the economic planners of the country as a whole. This study is helpful to different commercial banks, cooperatives who are providing finance to the fishermen of the district. Further, the study will also throw light on fishermen and the financial institutions to take various steps for proper utilization of fund.

Scope for Further Research

The study is confined to fishermen of Ganjam district relating to marine and inland fishing. It is mainly explanatory in nature. Further, a sample of 1200 fishermen are taken into account which is too small to come to a conclusion. Hence, the findings of the sample study does not guarantee hundred per cent accuracy with the parametric values of the universe. In addition, the statistical tools like probability, regeression analysis and other tests of large samples have not been applied. Hence further study in the subject is required. Some of the areas that need further study are:

(*i*) The study is confined to Ganjam district of Orissa. Therefore, the scope of the study can be extended to the entire State.

(*ii*) The study can be expanded by taking a large number of samples for better generalization and to make the analysis more comprehensive.

(*iii*) The present study is mainly confined to know the development of socio-economic condition of the fishermen borrowing loans. The problems faced by the government, financial institutions are not taken into consideration. Thus these can be taken as further research in this field.

Bibliography

1. Books

Agrawal, S.C. *Fishery Management*, Asis Publishing House, New Delhi, 1990.

Anderson, L.G. *Economic Impacts of Externded Fisheries Jurisdiction*, Ann Arbor Science Publishers, Michigan, 1977.

Bhattacharya, S.N. *Fisheries in Indian Economy*, Delhi Book Publishers, Delhi, 1965.

Bichwal, N. "Trends of Marine Fishery Production in India", Bombay Book Publishing House, Bombay, 1961.

Brandt, A.V. "*Fish Catching Methods of the World*", Fishing New Books Publishers Ltd., London, 1964.

Badapanda, H.S. "*Studies on Chilka Lake; Milestones*". Published in Fishing Chimes, Vol. 18, No. 8, Chimes House, Visakhapatnam, Andhra Pradesh, 1998.

Bal, D.V. and Rao, V.K. "*Marine Fisheries of India*", Tata McGraw-Hill Publishing Company Ltd., New Delhi, 1990.

Christy, F.T. and Scott, A.D. "*The Common Wealth in Ocean Fisheries*", John Hopkins Press, Baltimore, 1965.

Dhar, P.K. "*Indian Economy its Growing Dimension*", Kalyani Publishers, Cuttack, 2004.

Gupta, V.K. et al. "*Marine Fish Marketing in India*", IIM, Publications, Ahmedabad, 1983.

Gordon and Natarajan, "*Commercial Banking,*" Himalaya Publishing House, Hyderabad, 2006.

Holmgren, S *An Environmental Assessment of Bay of* Bengal Region", BOBP Publication, Madras, 1994.

Ibrahim, P., "Fisheries Development in India", Classical Publications, New Delhi, 1992.

Jhingran, G.V. "Fish and Fisheries of India", *The Journal of the Asiatic Society Bay of Bengal*, Vol. 19, No. 2, 1983.

Korkandy, R. Technological Change and the Development of Marine Fishing Industry in India, Daya Prublishing House, Delhi, 1994.

Khan, R. "*Indian Ocean Fisheries*", Ankur Publishing House, New Delhi, 1977.

Lahari, D, "*Role of fisheries in Rural Development*", Daya Publishing House, Delhi, 1994.

Lawson, R.M. "*Economics of Fisheries Development*", Francis Printer Puublishers, London, 1984.

Mamoria, C.B. "*Fisheries Problems of India*", Kitab Mahal, Allahabad, 1982.

Misra, P.M. "*Present Status an Future Prospects* of Fisheries in Orissa", Dept. of Marine Science, Berhampur University, Orissa, 1982.

Mishra, P.M. "*Marine Fishery Resources of India*", published by Department of Marine Science, Berhampur University, Orissa, 1988.

Mitra, G.N. and Mahapatra P. Bulletin on the Development of Chilka Lake-Survey Report on the Fishing Industry. Published by Orissa Government Press, Cuttack, 1957.

Morgan, R. "World Sea Fisheries", Mithaen and Company Ltd. London, 1956.

Norman, J.P. "A History of Fishes", Ernest Benn Ltd. London, 1963.

Osada and Nanda, "Traditional Fishing Gear in Developing Countries", FAO, Publication, Rome, 1996.

Panikar, J.K., "Marketing Channels of Marine Fish in India", Ashish Publishing House, New Delhi, 1990.

Paul M.J. *et al.*, "Explaining Public Support for Fisheries Alternatives", in the North American Journal of Fisheries Management, the American Fisheries Society, 1996.

Philippe, J., *et al.*, "Technology, Credit and Indebtedness in Marine Fishing", Hindustan Publishing Corporation, India, 1985.

Pramanik, S.K., *Fishermen Community in Coastal Villages of West Bengal*, Rawat Publications, New Delhi, 1993.

Rao, P.S., "Fishery Economics and Management in India", Pioneer Publishers and Distributors, Bombay, 1983.

Rao, S.N., "Fishery Development and Management in India", Northern Book Centre, New Delhi, 1986.

Ricker, S. "Biological Statistics of Fish and Models for their Sustainable Development", West View Press, Colorado, 1975.

Sahu, P. and Pradhan, N.N. *Fisheries Co-operatives in Orissa, A Case study of Financing BLC's in Ganjam District,* Discovery Publishing House, New Delhi, 1998.

Srivastava, C.B.L, "A Textbook on Fisheries Science and Indian Fisheries", Kitab Mahal, Ahmedabad, 1985.

Srivastava, U.K. and Dharma Reddy, M., "Fishery Development in India", Concept Publishing Company, New Delhi, 1984.

Srivastava, U.K. and Dharma Reddy, M. "*Management of Marine Fishing Industry*". Oxford and IBH Publishing Company, New Delhi, 1982.

Srivastava, U.K. et al., *Fishery Sector in India*, IIM, Ahmedabad, 1991.

Subba Rao, N. "*Economics of Fisheries, A Case Study of Andhra* Pradesh", Daya Publishing House, New Delhi, 1987.

Subba Rao, N. "Mechanisation and Marine Fishermen, A Case Study of Visakhapatnam". Northern Book Centre, New Delhi, 1996.

Taivo, L. and Felix. F. *Fishing and Stock Fluctuations*, Fishing New Books Ltd., England, 1989.

Tietze, U. and Kalavathy. *Artisanal Marine Fisherfolk of Orissa,* Vidyapuri Publications, Cuttack, 1994.

Tomczak, H.G. *Environmental Analysis in Marine Fisheries Research*, FAO Publications, Rome, 1977.

Theses

Aleyamma, Issac : "The economy of the marine higher women in Ganjam district in Orissa", 2000, Berhampur University.

Supriya, Bala "Economics of Marine Fisheries in Orissa", 1999, Berhampur University.

Mishra, Ava "The Socio-Economic Conditions of Chilika Fishermen—A Study of their Problems and Prospects", 1998, Berhampur University.

Sahu, Purussotam "Marine Fishing and Sustainable Development of the Fishermen in Ganjam District, Orissa", 2004, Berhampur University.

Bisoyi, T.K. "Credit Marketing Linkage of Marine Fisheries in Ganjam District, Orissa", 1991, Berhampur University.

Mahaprasasta, J. "Credit Marketing Linkage of Fishing at Chilika: A Case Study of a Village" 1990, Berhampur University.

3. Articles

Ali, S.M. "Marine Fisheries of Orissa State, Current Status and Future Prospects." *Journal of Fisheries Economics and Development*, Vol. 2, No. 1, Hydereabad, 1995.

Anderson, I.G. Enhancing Economic Analysis for Fisheries Management Discussion". *American Journal of Agricultural Economics*, Vol. 75(5), 1993.

Aqua International, Vol. 5 No. (3 & 4) (7 & 8). A Magazine of W.R.S. Publications Hyderabad, 1997.

Aqua International, "A Monthly on Aqua and Marine Industry" Vol. 6, No. 9. A Magazine of NRS Publications, Hyderabad, 1999.

Alappat, B.J. *et al.*, "Threats to the Marine Environment", *Yojana*, September, 1998.

Bhullar, K.S. "Credit for Fishing Industry", *Sea food Export Journal*, Vol. 4, No. 1, Cochin, 1974.

Bay of Bengal News, The Journal of BOBP for Fisheries Management, Vol. 11. No. 2, 3 (1996) 5, 6, 7, 8 (1997), 9, 10, 12 (1998) and 13, 14 (1999), Published by BOBP, Chennai.

Cedernet, "Saving People of Chilka" SWEDMER, *Journal of Sweden*, 1992.

Cheston, C. "Export, Out look for Indian Marine Products", Vol. 49, No. 7, *Sea Food Export Journal*, 1983.

Chong, K.C. "Small-scale Fisheries in the Bay of Bengal Region: New Opportunities in New Century". Vol. 13, *BOBP News*, BOBP, Chennai, 1999.

Chong, K.C. "Responsible Fish consumers can strengthen Fisheries Management" Vol. 11(3), *The Journal of BOBP*, Chennai, 1996.

Choudhry, R.P. and Nayak, H. (1995), "Aquaculture and its Infrastructural Development in Orissa", *The Orissa Journal of Commerce,* Vol. XIX.

Custing, D. "Fisheries Resources of the sea and their Management- A Study of Irrational Conservation", Vol.52, No.3 *American Journal of Agricultural Economics,* 1970.

Davis. J. "Managing our Oceans for Mankind", Vol. 30, No. 12, *Journal of Fisheries Research Board,* Canada, 1973.

Garrod, D.J. "Management of Multipurpose Resources", Vol. 30 (12) *Journal of Fishery Research Board,* Canada, 1973.

George, P.C. "Some thoughts of Maximum Utilisation of Coastal Fishery Resource of India", Vol.5, No.1 & 2 Journal of Indian Fisheries Association, Bombay, 1975.Gorden, H.S. "An Economic Approach to the Optimum Utilisation of Fisheries Resources", Vol. 10, *Journal of Fisheries Research Board, Canada,* 1954.

Gorden, H.S. "Economic Theory of a Common Property Resource: The Fishery" 62(2), *Journal of Political Economics,* 1954.

Henderson, J. V. and Tugwell, M. "Exploitation of the Lobster Fishery. Some Empirical Results", *Journal of Environmental Economics & Management,* 1979.

Hora, S.L. "Knowledge of the Ancient Hindu Concerning Fish and Fisheries of India", Vol. 16(1), *Journal of the Asiatics Society,* 1950.

Jakis, M.P. Fly, J.M. and Wilson, J.L. "Explaining Public Support for Fisheries Management Alternatives", Vol. 16(1), *North American Journal of Fisheries Mangement,* USA, 1996.

James, P.S.B.R. "Prospects of Rising Marinal Fish Production in India Through Rational Exploitation of the EEZ", *Souvenir, Asian Fisheries Society,* Mangalore, 1987.

Job. T.J. and Pantulu, V.R. "Fish Trapping in India". Vol. 19, No. 2, *The Journal of the Asiatic Society,* Bay of Bengal, 1958.

Kokate, K.D. and Upare, S.M. (2005), "Role of Fisheries in Rural Development", *Kurukshetra,* 53 (8).

Krishnamurty, B. "An Assessment of the Demersal Fishery Resources of the Andhra-Orissa Coast based on Exploratory Trawling, "Vol. 21(2), *Indian Journal of Fisheries,* 1976.

Kurin, J. "Entry of Big Business into Fishing, It's impact on Fish Economy", Vol. 13, No. 36, *Economic and Political Weekly,* 1978.

Mishra, P.M. "Sea food for Orissa, Their Export Potential and Internal Demand", *Seafood Export Journal*, Cochin, 1975.

Mishra, Rabinarayam, (2005) or Development of Production of Fish in Fresh water in Orissa", *Yojana,* (July).

Misra, R.N. (2003), "Stock of water for Fish Cultivation", *Yojana,* 12 (9).

Mitra, G.N. "The Task Before the Central Marine Fisheries Research of India". *Souvenir,* CMFRI, Cochin, 1986.

Muthiah, S. "God and the Diminishing Fisheries Resources" *Bay of Bengal News,* Chennai, 1991.

Nair, P.M. "Fisheries for the Future", Vol. 8, No. 2, *Fisheries Journal,* 1993.

Nanda, S. "More on Externalities in the Fishery; A Discussion of Economic Efficiency", Vol. 32(3). *The Indian Economic Journal,* 1985.

Qasim, S.Z. "Some Projections of Marine Living Resources in the year 2000 A.D." *Souvenir, CMFRI,* Cochin, 1986.

Rao, P.S. "Price Policy for Marine Fish" Vol. 3, No. 5, *Sea food Export Journal, Cochin,* 1971. rf.

Ray, A.B. "Marine Fisheries Potential of Orissa and its Scope for Exploitation", Vol. 7, No. 9, *Seafood Export Journal,* 1975.

Sahes, Anil Kumar and Nayale, S.S. (2005), "Fisheris in Orissa?: A Management Look", *Journal ofcommerce and Economics,* vol., xiv.

Saxena, B.S. "Indian Fisheries in the National Economy", Vol. 23, No. 4, *Indian Journal of Agricultural Economics*, 1968.

Smith, V.L. "On Models of Commercial Fishing" Vol. 77, No. 6, *Journal of Political Economy,* 1969.

Tharakan, A.J. "An Action Plan for Sea Food Exporting", Vol. 25, No. 4, *Seafood Export Journal,* Cochin, 1998.

Valliammai, A. and Thanganuthes, (2004) "Environemental Issue in Poawn Culture", *Yojana,* 48 (6).

Reports

Ahmed, N.K. A "*Report on Fishery, Hydrographic and Meteorological Profile of the Coast of Orissa*". Directorate of Fisheries, Cuttack, 1993.

Ann Gorden Inferstate Marketing Linkages (CMFRI), Report, Vol. 68, Cochin, 1997.

Annual Report of Andhra Bank 1999-2005.

Annual Report of Co-operative Banks 2003-05

Annual Report of Major Exporting Firms 2000-04, Marine Products Export Development Agency, Bhubaneswar, Orissa.

Annual Report of RGB-1990-2005

Annual Reports of NABARD 2001-2005, NABARD Press, Bhubaneswar, Orissa.

Banking Statstics-1992-93 to 2003-04, Reserve Bank of India.

BOBP report-73 "*Coastal Fisheries Management.* BOBP, Chennai, 1996.

BOBP, Report 75, "*Coastal Resources Management System*" BOBP, Chennai, 1997.

"Interstate Marketing Linkages", *CMFRI*, Vol. 68, Cochin.

Orissa State Assembly Report on Fisheries, Development of Orissa, Dharitri-27.8.05

Potential linked Credit Plan for Ganjam District, NABARD, Orissa, 2006-07.

"Potention linked Credit Plan for Orissa", NABARD, Bhubaneswar, Orissa (2006).

Raja. B.T.A. Orissa Fisheries "Astrang Harbour Project". CMFRI, Publication, Cochin.

Report of the Regional Workshop on the Precautionary Approach to Fisheries Management, BOBP, Chennai, India, 1999.

Report of the Workshop on Smart Partnership for Sustainability in the Fishing Industries, BOBP, Chennai, India, 1999.

Report on Brackish Water Aquaculture, CIFA, Bhubaneswar, 1998.

Report on Marketing of the Marine and Brackish Water Fish in West Bengal and Orissa, BOBP Internal Report, Chennai.

SLBC (State Level Bankers Committee Report), 2005-06.

Socio-Economics of Artisanal Marine Fisheries Along Ganjam Coast, OUAT, Rangailunda, Orissa.

Government Publications

"A study of the Marine Fishery Resources of Orissa"—Published by FSI, Bombay, Dept. of Agriculture Co-operation, Government of India.

All India Census Report, 2001, Government of India.

Chopra, B.N. "*Handbook of Indian Fisheries*", Government of India Press, New Delhi. 1951.

Directorate of Fisheries, "*Orissa Fisheries at a Glance*", Government of Orissa, Cuttack-2001.

Districts at a Glance, 1998-2005, Government of Orissa, Bhubaneswar.

Economic Survey 1997-98 to 2005-06, Government of Orissa, Bhubaneswar.

Government of India, "*Hand book of Indian Fisheries, Statistics*" Published by Ministry of Agriculture, Government of India, New Delhi, 2005.

Government of Orissa, "*Eight Plan 1992-97*" Vol. 1, Planning and Co-ordination Dept. Government of Orissa, Cuttack, 1991.

Hand book of Indian Fisheries, Statistics 2005, Published by Ministery of Agriculture, Government of India, New Delhi.

Hand book of Indian Fisheries, Government of India Press, New Delhi.

Hand Book on Fisheries Statistics, Orissa, (2001) Director of Fishereis, Government of Orissa, Cuttack.

Kurukshetra (2004-06) Information and Broad Casting Department, New Delhi.

OSFC, "Position Paper on Trawleers' Cuttack, Government of Orissa, 1981.

Orissa Fisheries at a Glance Director of Fisheries Government of Orissa Cuttack.

Stastical Abstract Government of India, New Delhi, 1999-2000.

Stastical Abstract of Orissa, 2005, Government of Orissa, Bhubaneswar

Yojana (2003-05) Information and Broad Casting Department, New Delhi.

Index

S

T

V

W

❑❑❑